The DevOps Assessment

Playbook

A Comprehensive Assessment Primer to assess Technology Organizations for DevOps

URMILA KANDHA

Author of "Essentials of Agile Transformation"

The DevOps Assessment Playbook

1st Edition

Publication Date: July 2019

Price: ₹999 | $18.99

ISBN: 978-93-88644-28-0

Published by:

Adhyyan Books
Office No. 637,
Opposite Vivanta by Taj,
DDA SFS. Pocket-1, Dwarka,
Sec-22, New Delhi-110077
Website: www.adhyyanbooks.com

E-mail: contact@adhyyanbooks.com

This book is dedicated to my ever encouraging and loving parents, Narayandas and Kalpana Naidu who have always stood by me in helping me accomplish my dreams and to the loving memories of my late grandma Rangamani Naidu, who has a profound influence in holding the clay of my thoughts and enabling me to craft my passion to reality!
Dadi, how I wish you were there to witness this book unfold in your hands!

Special Thanks

No matter what roles we play in our professional space, we are humans in reality. We all share emotions and need people who understand, inspire, empathize and drive us through the hills and valleys of difficult situations in life while we continue to fight our personal battles. This book to me is a precious gift that I thank the Divine for enabling my energies to finish through completion. Apart from my family who has always stood steadfastly in all times, there have been special angels whom I can't stop enough to express gratitude for.

Hrishikesh Karekar, my mentor, who strongly helped me clear the fog through challenged times and enabled me finish this project to the last mile when I suffered with some serious health issues while writing this book. The one person who trusted "I can do it" even when I lost trust on myself. The one person whom I see as a coach, a mentor and a true guru. Someone who enabled me to be more vocal in analyzing priorities, establish balance with myself, meet all my professional commitments without guilt and at the same time achieve my personal vision. Someone who spared time to stand by during unforgettable situations, break the writer's kryptonite and rebuild the lost confidence. There are times I got scolded too. Not to forget. But when you understand the intent and objective of that scolding, you realize the good behind it. Bouncing ideas with Hrishi is a sure avenue to learn endlessly.

Every trait of emotional agility and transformational leadership that I read or listen resonates with him with profound examples. Even eagles need a push to fly, then why not humans. They say that true leadership is not being in charge but taking care of those in charge. And transformational leaders take that extra mile to inspire, encourage, mentor and help their teams accomplish their personal vision. Hrishi– thank you for making that immense difference and enabling me to schedule my dream into reality. You can never be thanked enough. I must say that God sends people to represent Him when I read footprints on the sands of time and I do not have words beyond this for such leadership.

Contents

About the Author .... *xv*
Foreword .... *xvii*
Who should read this book? .... *xix*
Key Takeaways .... *xix*
How is the book structured? .... *xx*
Preface .... *xxv*

Part 1 .... *01*
Introduction *03*
The DevOps Lifestyle ***06***
What is DevOps? *06*
Why DevOps? *06*
How to embrace DevOps? *08*
Budgeting for DevOps *09*
Assessing DevOps *11*
What is a DevOps Assessment? *11*
Why do enterprises need a DevOps Assessment? *11*
What to ask prior to starting an Enterprise DevOps Assessment? *13*
How long does it take for a DevOps Assessment? *15*
What is the support needed from the Assessee Organization for a DevOps Assessment? *18*
Manpower / Skills needed for conducting a DevOps Assessment *18*
Outcomes of a DevOps Assessment *19*
How is a DevOps Assessment Structured? *20*
Assessment Focus areas *21*
Selecting Pilot Candidates for Assessment *21*
Assessment, Scope and Coverage *23*
Focus Groups *25*
Collecting Assessment Data *25*

Part 2 .... *27*
Leadership and Commitment *29*
Leadership and Commitment for Business Transformation ***31***
- *Assessment Objectives* *31*
- *Key Practices Summary* *32*

Leadership Agility 33
Why Assess? 33
Key Practice Summry 33
Assessment Questions 34
Leaders Think 35
Strategy, Vision and Goals 36
Why Assess? 36
Key Practice Summary 36
Assessment questions 37
Leaders Think 38
Change Ambassadors Agility 40
Why Assess? 40
Key Practice Summary 40
Assessment questions 40
Leaders Think 42
DevOps Team Topology 43
Why Assess? 43
Key Practice Summary 43
Assessment questions 44
Leaders Think 45
Innovation 46
Why Assess? 46
Key Practice Summary 46
Assessment questions 47
Leaders Think 48

Organization , Team and Culture 49
Organization Design and its influence on Business Transformation 51
Assessment Objectives 51
Key Practices Summary 52
Team Empowerment and Autonomy 53
Why Assess? 53
Key Practice Summary 53
Assessment questions 54
Leaders Think 55
Immersive Learning 56
Why Assess? 56
Key Practice Summary 56
Assessment questions 57

Leaders Think ... 58
DOJOs ... 60
Why Assess? ... 60
Key Practice Summary ... 60
Assessment questions ... 61
Leaders Think ... 61
Adaptive Release Planning and Orchestration ... 62
Why Assess? ... 62
Key Practice Summary ... 63
Assessment questions ... 63
Leaders Think ... 65
Metrics ... 66
Why Assess? ... 66
Key Practice Summary ... 66
Assessment questions ... 67
Leaders Think ... 68
Organization Design for Collaboration at Scale ... 69
Why Assess? ... 69
Key Practice Summary ... 69
Assessment questions ... 70
Leaders Think ... 71
DevOps Contracting Models ... 72
Why Assess? ... 72
Key Practice Summary ... 73
Assessment questions ... 73
Leaders Think ... 74

Technical Practices, Tools and Processes ... 75
Why Technical Practices, Tools and Processes matter to DevOps? ... 77
Assessment Objectives ... 77
Key Practices Summary ... 77
Technical Debt Management ... 78
Why Assess? ... 78
Key Practice Summary ... 78
Assessment questions ... 79
Leaders Think ... 80
Source Control Management ... 81
Why Assess? ... 81
Key Practice Summary ... 81

Assessment questions 82
Leaders Think 83
Build Management **84**
Why Assess? 84
Key Practice Summary 84
Assessment questions 85
Leaders Think 85
Test Management **86**
Why Assess? 86
Key Practice Summary 86
Assessment questions 87
Leaders Think 88
Emergent Design **89**
Why Assess? 89
Key Practice Summary 89
Assessment questions 90
Leaders Think 91
Scriptless Automation and Jobs-as-Code **92**
Why Assess? 92
Key Practice Summary 92
Assessment questions 93
Leaders Think 94
Automated Environment Provisioning **95**
Why Assess? 95
Key Practice Summary 96
Assessment questions 96
Leaders Think 97
Continuous Quality with Smart Toolchains **100**
Why Assess? 100
Key Practice Summary 101
Assessment Questions 101
Leaders Think 102
Continuous Integration **103**
Why Assess? 103
Key Practice Summary 103
Assessment Questions 104
Leaders Think 105
Continuous Testing **106**
Why Assess? 106

Key Practice Summary *106*
Assessment Questions *107*
Leaders Think *107*
Continuous Monitoring ***109***
Why Assess? *109*
Key Practice Summary *110*
Assessment Questions *110*
Leaders Think *111*
Telemetry ***112***
Why Assess? *112*
Key Practice Summary *112*
Assessment Questions *113*
Leaders Think *113*
Continuous Delivery and Deployment ***114***
Why Assess? *114*
Key Practice Summary *114*
Assessment Questions *115*
Leaders Think *116*

Infrastructure **117**
Role of Infrastructure in a DevOps Transformation ***119***
Assessment Objectives *119*
Key Practices Summary *120*
Infrastructure as Code ***121***
Why Assess? *121*
Key Practice Summary *122*
Assessment Questions *122*
Leaders Think *123*
REST API Management ***124***
Why Assess? *124*
Key Practice Summary *124*
Assessment Questions *125*
Leaders Think *125*
Microservices ***126***
Why Assess? *126*
Key Practice Summary *126*
Assessment Questions *127*
Leaders Think *127*
AIOps ***129***

Why Assess? *129*
Key Practice Summary *129*
Assessment Questions *130*
Leaders Think *130*
Immutable Infrastructure ***132***
Why Assess? *132*
Why are containers popular towards Immutable Infrastructure? *132*
Key Benefits of Immutable Infrastructure *133*
Key Practice Summary *133*
Assessment Questions *134*
Leaders Think *134*
Cloud Bursting ***135***
Why Assess? *135*
Key Practice Summary *136*
Assessment Questions *136*
Leaders Think *137*
Self-healing Application Design ***138***
Why Assess? *138*
Key Practice Summary *138*
Assessment Questions *139*
Leaders Think *139*
ChatOps ***140***
Why Assess? *141*
Key Practice Summary *142*
Assessment Questions *142*
Leaders Think *143*

Security **145**
Role of Security in DevOps ***147***
DevSecOps ***147***
Key Assessment Objectives *147*
Key Practices Summary *148*
Security as Code ***149***
Why Assess? *149*
Key Practice Summary *149*
Assessment Questions *150*
Leaders Think *151*
Data and Application Security ***152***
Why Assess? *152*

Key Practice Summary *152*
Assessment Questions *152*
Leaders Think *153*
Container Security ***155***
Why Assess? *155*
Key Practice Summary *155*
Assessment Questions *156*
Leaders Think *157*
Network Security ***158***
Why Assess? *158*
Key Practice Summary *158*
Assessment Questions *159*
Leaders Think *159*
Automated Security Testing ***160***
Why Assess? *160*
Key Practice Summary *160*
Assessment Questions *161*
Leaders Think *161*
Right Touch Regulation ***162***
Why Assess? *162*
Key Practice Summary *162*
Assessment Questions *163*
Leaders Think *163*
Security Assurance ***164***
Why Assess? *164*
Key Practice Summary *164*
Assessment Questions *165*
Leaders Think *166*
Vulnerability Management ***167***
Why Assess? *167*
Key Practice Summary *167*
Assessment Questions *168*
Leaders Think *168*
Continuous Compliance ***169***
Why Assess? *169*
Key Practice Summary *169*
Assessment Questions *170*
Leaders Think *170*

Part 3 .... **171**
Assessment Outcomes **173**
Assessment Scoring and Analysis *175*
Key Deliverables from an Assessment *176*
What to expect in a Recommendations Report *176*
What NOT to expect in a Recommendations Report *177*
DevOps Assessment Report *177*

Transformation Roadmap and ROI **181**
DevOps Transformation Roadmap *183*
Why Prepare a Transformation Roadmap for DevOps? *183*
How to Create a Transformation Roadmap? *183*
Developing a DevOps Progression Model *186*
Assessing ROI from DevOps *187*
ROI Projections at Project (rather Product) Level *188*
ROI Projections at Portfolio, Line of Business or Organizational Level ... *192*
How is DevOps for Digital different from DevOps for legacy systems? *194*
Workforce Transformation for DevOps *195*

Critical Success Factors for DevOps Transformation **199**
The Secret Sauce to Successful DevOps Transformation ***206***

Conclusion **209**

List of Abbreviations *213*
Bibliography *217*
Acknowledgements *221*
Endorsements *225*

About the Author

Urmila Kandha, author of ***"Essentials of Agile Transformation"*** has 19+ years of industry experience graduating from a programmer to an enterprise Agile and DevOps advisor. Presently a Transformation Leader with Capgemini, her prior experience includes her association with Deutsche Bank Group, Cognizant Technology Solutions, Infosys Technologies, Covansys and Tata Consultancy Services.

She has been an ardent thought leader, entrepreneur and a keynote speaker at multiple Agile and DevOps conferences globally with multiple whitepapers to her credit. Urmila is also the spiral lead for "Lean-In Agile," a movement oriented to empower women and build the learner's league collaboratively. In her leisure, Urmila mentors forward-thinking practitioners and aspiring authors to realize their passionate ambitions.

Foreword

Keeping up with the accelerated maturity of computing is an arduous task. The first programming language—Plankalkül—was developed in 1944 and the first transistor was demonstrated at Bell Laboratories in December of 1947. To put such acceleration into perspective, consider that the Renaissance lasted around 300 years and the industrial revolution lasted about 200 years.

In less than 80 years we have gone from ENIAC's 5,000 addition calculations per second to Ryzen™ 7's 304.5 million instructions per second. Programming has gone from procedural to structured, object-oriented to refinements such as clean code. But that isn't enough to keep up with today's world. Computing and the internet have expanded the reach of technology to virtually all people on the planet. Social media and more recently Internet of Things are changing the way we live, the way we do things and the way we see the world.

The Renaissance started with Humanism, the idea that man is the center of its own universe and therefore embraced education, arts, science and literature. Computing and software are now at the point where the focus is shifting from the technology itself to humanism, where the focus is on how to apply technology to improve the way we live and interact. Arguably, software development humanism started with the advent of the Agile Manifesto in 2001, which is maturing the way we develop software products and manage software projects. In 2008, Patric Debois and Andrew Clay Shafer proposed an extension of agile to include infrastructure and the first DevOps conference was held in Ghent, Belgium.

Nowadays DevOps is popularizing faster than Agile, in part thanks to Agile's accelerated popularization. In practice, there are two prevalent behaviours. Some organizations are adopting DevOps in a hurry and others are doing DevOps by name but not in practice. It will be of great benefit to such organizations to get a clear picture of where they really are in their adoption of DevOps or to know what their state of DevOps really is if the adoption has been already done.

Urmila, whom I've known for over two years, has a well-rooted practical approach to managing organizations as it is demonstrated on her book on "Essentials of Agile Transformation", where she addresses the humanistic side of Agile and cultural aspects essential for a successful agile transformation. A smart move was to include opinions of world experts.

On this book on DevOps Assessments, Urmila continues her practical approach by providing you with a comprehensive guide to determine the state of DevOps at your organization. To make your life easier, it is divided into five top-down areas that include the humanistic side of DevOps—which is the most important aspect of DevOps and not the tools and techniques as most implementations wrongfully consider—from leadership to culture, the organization and teams, to then address the technical aspects. The book includes a chapter on DevSecOps, which is very important for organizations of all kinds and a chapter on how to analyze your assessment.

Urmila doesn't claim this book to be a complete assessment guide but rather a comprehensive one form which you have to determine what to apply at your organization.

This is a time-saver guide useful before, during and after the assessment. I foresee this book at many decision-makers' desk with the pages worn out after being consulted time and again. Quite useful on today's rapidly maturing software development and operations.

Masa K. Maeda, PhD

CEO, Valueinnova LLC

Utah, USA.

Who should read this book?

The primary audience for this book is all strategic leaders in technology organizations who have embraced the transformation journey with DevOps. It is also a valuable asset to consultants and coaches who are facilitating such organizations in realizing their ambitions of DevOps organizations.

A secondary read is for all startups who are also hopping on the DevOps bandwagon in terms of aggressively achieving their strategic goals while staying lean and nimble on structure and delivery. In short, this book is for any leader or consultant who wants to understand and assess enterprise readiness and maturity for DevOps and design the enterprise for DevOps in a structured manner.

Key Takeaways

This book contains more than 500 questions from actual assessments executed for various organizations across domains, geographies and lines of businesses ranging from startups to some of the large-sized enterprises.

Read this book to

- Understand what a DevOps Assessment means for an enterprise
- What are its dimensions?
- Whom should you assess and what should ask?
- How do you select pilot candidates for Assessment?
- Where do you start your journey?
- How to do an Assessment?
- How to craft a DevOps Assessment Report?
- What are some of the typical outcomes achieved?
- How do you prioritize the solutions and arrive at a Transformation Roadmap for DevOps?
- How do you assess the ROI from your transformation?

- How do you leverage the Assessment outcomes to guide the organization with its DevOps strategy?

And much more…

Isn't all this the strategy consulting that you were looking for? The outcomes of the assessment enable you to create a transformation roadmap and choose the near term and long term goals. In a nutshell, it will help you establish a data-driven DevOps transformation strategy.

Read this to navigate through the above and gain much more.

How is the book structured?

The book lays down the cornerstones for DevOps Assessment in the below five focus areas

1. Leadership and Commitment
2. Organization, Team and Culture
3. Technical Practices, Tools and Processes
4. Infrastructure
5. Security

Each of these areas has multiple key practices that will delve into the details for further assessment. A big picture representation of the structure of this book is shown in the following view.

A DevOps Assessment Canvas also feeds into the organization's DevOps Strategy. A summarized view of the same is depicted in the following picture. This book covers all these areas and as a business leader or strategy consultant, you may pick and choose to read those sections of the book that entice you the most.

The DevOps Assessment Big Picture

D1-DevOps Mindset
D2-DevOps Culture
D3-Organization Design for DevOps
D4-Continuous Learning
D5-Continuous Integration, Delivery and Deployment
D6-Continuous Monitoring
D7-DevOps Infrastructure
D8-Continuous Security

Focus Area	Key Practice	DevOps Disciplines							
		D1	D2	D3	D4	D5	D6	D7	D8
Leadership & Commitment	Leadership Agility	√	√						
	Strategy, Vision and Goals	√	√						
	Change Ambassadors Agility	√	√						
	DevOps Team Topology		√	√					
	Innovation	√	√	√					
Organization, Team & Culture	Team Empowerment and Autonomy		√	√					
	Immersive Learning			√	√				
	DOJOs		√	√	√				
	Adaptive Release Planning and Orchestration		√	√					
	Metrics	√	√	√	√				
	Organization Design for Collaboration at Scale			√					
	DevOps Contracting Models			√					
Technical Practices, Tools & Processes	Technical Debt Management			√					
	Source Control Management			√	√	√	√		√
	Build Management			√	√	√	√		√
	Test Management			√	√	√	√		√
	Emergent Design			√	√	√	√		√
	Scriptless Automation and Jobs-as-Code			√	√	√	√		√
	Automated Environment Provisioning			√	√		√	√	√
	Continuous Quality with Smart Toolchains			√					
	Continuous Integration			√	√	√			
	Continuous Testing			√		√			
	Telemetry			√			√		
	Continuous Monitoring			√			√		
	Continuous Delivery and Deployment			√		√			√

The DevOps Assessment Big Picture

D1-DevOps Mindset
D2-DevOps Culture
D3-Organization Design for DevOps
D4-Continuous Learning
D5-Continuous Integration, Delivery and Deployment
D6-Continuous Monitoring
D7-DevOps Infrastructure
D8-Continuous Security

Focus Area	Key Practice	DevOps Disciplines							
		D1	D2	D3	D4	D5	D6	D7	D8
Infrastructure	Infrastructure as Code			√				√	
	REST API Management			√					
	Microservices			√					
	AIOps			√				√	
	Immutable Infrastructure			√				√	
	Cloud Bursting			√				√	
	Self-healing Application Design			√				√	
	ChatOps			√				√	
Security	Security as Code			√					√
	Data and Application Security			√					√
	Container Security			√					√
	Network Security			√					√
	Automated Security Testing			√					√
	Right Touch Regulation			√					√
	Security Assurance			√					√
	Vulnerability Management			√					√
	Continuous Compliance			√					√

As a reader, you can go through these sections in the order of what entices you the most.

If you are an application team member and interested in improving your technical practices and processes, the sections on Organization, team and culture and Technical practices, tools and processes are most appropriate to you.

If you are an infrastructure specialist and interested in understanding what DevOps means in terms of being assessed, go through the section on Infrastructure to get more details.

If you are a security expert and interested in understanding what DevSecOps means in terms of being assessed, go through the relevant section.

If you are a transformation leader or consultant and are assessing your organization, every section of this book is relevant to you.

The last three chapters are for anyone who would like to understand how the data gathered from conversations will get analyzed for action. These also take it one step further and give details on how a transformation roadmap for the organization can be created and near-term and long-term actions can be strategically prioritized, how you would assess ROI from your transformation and some critical success factors for a DevOps transformation.

A DevOps Assessment Canvas also feeds into the organization's DevOps Strategy. A summarized view of the same is depicted in the following picture. This book covers all these areas and as a business leader or strategy consultant, you may pick and choose to read those sections of the book that entice you the most.

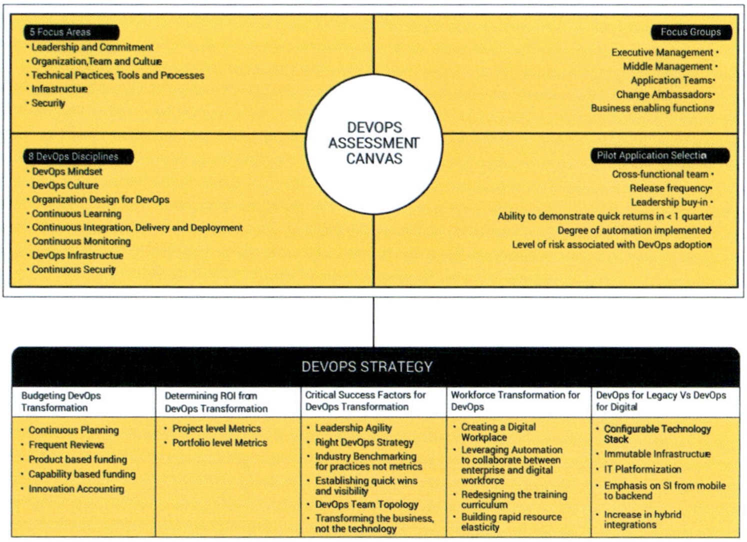

Preface

Assessments have always been a popular tool of choice when it comes to assessing how good or bad we are - our personal selves or organizations. I remember starting my journey with CMM assessments way back in the 90s - 2000 timeframe and then transitioning to CMMI, which then was squished away with the Agile Wave. DevOps takes it to the ultimate level by completing the thread of idea to deployment - including operations, infrastructure and all other support functions on top of the agile organization.

Irrespective of the Agile or DevOps capability maturity assessment models that are existent, as an industry, we still consistently find the same challenges in terms of how we should become more agile as an organization or embrace the DevOps Mindset. Through this book, I let you as a Transformation Leader or a Change Ambassador dig into the various pockets of organizations that need to be thought through from transforming the DevOps way. In other words, it is much beyond a mere set of tools that are synonymously linked with DevOps. Without the right amount of enablement on the human capital in terms of overall understanding this canvas, any amounts of investments in the technology space would be futile attempts to transform.

- How do you assess your readiness with Immutable Infrastructure?
- What is your readiness to embrace Security as Code?
- As an organization, what is the extent to which you have converted Jobs as Code?
- Have you thought of integrating ChatOps as part of your forward thinking Transformation Strategy?
- While scaling your infrastructure in virtual environments, with containerization and multi-tenancy paradigms, are you aligning the DevOps way influencing the Organization Design for DevOps?
- While scaling your infrastructure in virtual environments, with containerization and multi-tenancy paradigms, are you aligning the DevOps way influencing the Organization Design for DevOps?

It is these aspects that make this book uniquely poised from the perspective of triggering you as a transformation leader to think through the various aspects that need to be looked at in coherence in order to successfully transform with DevOps. Unless you do some retrospection and self-assess your strategic objectives and your organizational readiness and maturity for DevOps on a candid plane, you cannot align your transformation initiatives with organizational priorities. This is a playbook for all visionaries and game changers who are seated with a determination to make change happen!

Feliz lettura!

Part 1

Introduction

Introduction

Enterprises are going through continued turbulence in a VUCA (Volatile, Uncertain, Complex and Ambiguous) world today. With growing disruption in the technology and business landscape and fast-paced demands from customers, the speed of delivering change and harnessing it to business advantage is extremely critical for IT to thrive and flourish.

Most CIOs are struggling to deliver IT successfully with rapidly changing technology landscape, shift in business and operating models and rapidly changing business requirements from tech-savvy customers. Another key challenge is a lack of collaboration and cohesive alignment across IT teams, business stakeholders, end users and operations which places enterprises capabilities in a nebulous priority. All these challenges combined with an absence of a clear roadmap that sequences new capabilities in alignment with strategic priorities generally sub-optimize an organization's decisions around technology investments. It is here that CIOs choose to go digital building on world class and transformational business practices that require new ways of thinking to help streamline processes and optimize performance.

While there are multiple models and philosophies that help them meet these goals, DevOps is one of the best recommended for most such organizations. Used by many enterprises to achieve enhanced productivity, speedy delivery and provide greater value to customers through shorter time to market, DevOps is rapidly becoming the defacto gold standard of technology development. Most of the successful organizations like Amozon, Netflix and so on have rapidly delivered changes with predictability, speed, reliability and stability become market leaders have tried, tested and embraced DevOps to build speed, predictability and stability in their businesses by shortening the release cycle times and delivering business value in a more frequent and controlled manner.

So when you think of stepping on a DevOps journey, what all does come to your mind?

The DevOps Lifestyle

What is DevOps?

DevOps is a culture and a mindset that enables a set of processes that bring development and operations teams together to finish software development seamlessly in the most effective manner.

It allows organizations to get a competitive edge by improving the time to market and product release cycle times as compared to traditional software development approaches.

Building on enterprise agility, DevOps promotes active collaboration in the enterprise landscape influencing accelerated business value, shorter time to market and improved quality of software delivered. It is becoming the norm of modern day enterprises in the way they build systems and applications.

Software projects a decade ago were characterized by a huge bundle of requirements baselines and signed with a visibility to deliver in windows as long as an year or multiyear horizons. Today's software needs to been seen and felt on the go and continuously evolve with the changing needs of tech-savvy customers.

DevOps facilitates this by bringing together Development and Operations teams to acheive this mission in the most efficient manner leveraging tools and automation.

Why DevOps?

Embracing DevOps has multiple benefits for an organization

- Rapid and continuous deployment and close collaboration with the customer are hallmarks of DevOps practices
- Iterative and incremental deliveries with fast feedback from customer enhance the overall customer experience. This results in better release predictability through shorter release cycles and improved business value delivery to customers
- DevOps best practices speed up application delivery and businesses get products to market faster than with traditional methods
- DevOps practices enable increased collaboration amongst business, IT,

operations, suppliers and other business enabling functions that in turn make the delivery curve more efficient

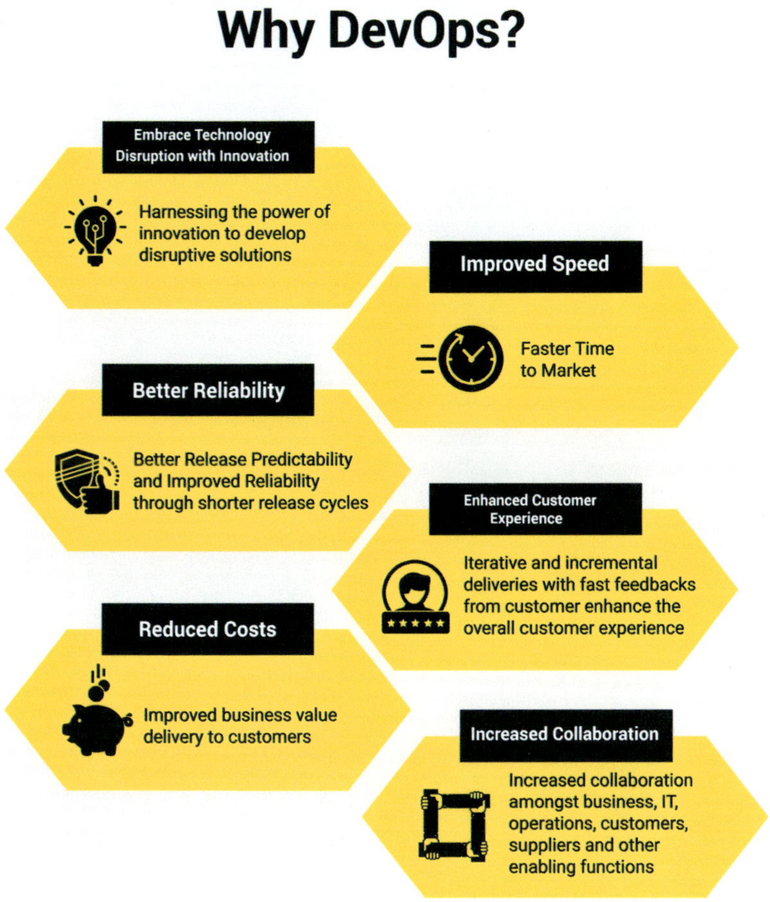

How to embrace DevOps?

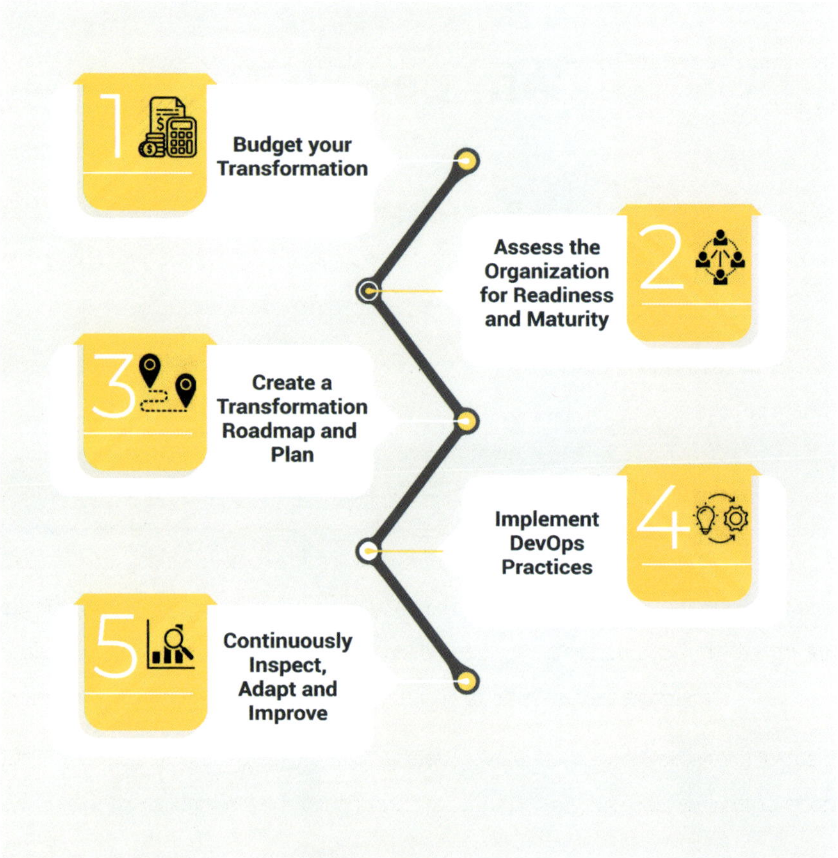

Embracing DevOps involves starting budgeting for the DevOps with an adaptive view to accommodate changes and reprioritize the funding. Continuous funding and continuous commitment from the management on how DevOps will help them meet their strategic prioritize or address their pain areas builds visibility for boarding the DevOps train in the organization and sets the pace to the entire transformation.

Budgeting for DevOps is different from traditional budgeting and is discussed in the subsequent section. The focus area of this book being the core assessment, the next sections explore all peripherals around it.

Budgeting for DevOps

When an enterprise chooses to transform the DevOps way, even the traditional ways of budgeting and funding need to change. CIOs cannot spend a year reconciling yesterday's budgetary predictions with an annual horizon that does not meet today's budgetary and funding needs. Organizational dynamics, re-structuring and alignment, personal agendas and power-play decisions can top up the complexity of traditional budgeting techniques. With many assumptions in hindsight and new risks, disruptions or opportunities uncovered, the budgeting exercise needs adaptability to meet the needs of DevOps.

Some of the popular budgeting models (to budget DevOps transformation) used by successful organization including startups and mid-to-large enterprises include the following elements.

- **Shorter budgetary cycles and frequent introspections**
  - This model still leverages the traditional contract of annual budgeting but introduces gates reviews at every quarter on rolling wave basis
  - Plans are continuously revisited jointly by traditional contract of annual usiness and IT and resources and funds are allocated based on repriortization decisions made for quarter.
  - Benefits of this model include lesser financial risk, improved visibility of the dynamic demands of a product, capability or service and flexibility to implement feature-based funding and MVPs thereby promoting value-driven delivery
  - Challenges of this model are that if it is not kept nimble and involves multi-tiered approvals for every single decision, then the benefits of the whole exercise are lost
- **Product or Capability-based funding**
  - The most common model that delegates budgetary decisions to the product owner who can choose to distribute the budget based on his financial assessment of the overall product portfolio

- Benefits of this model include siplicity and empowerment to the front line who can decide where to invest and where not to. This influences the timeto-market and product reliability too
- Risks of this model include the focus and attention on new features and services being devloped leaving maintenance and technical debt in hindsight
- Challenges of this model are that it needs the organization to acquire product thinking moving away from the typical project thinking. Acquiring a product mindset is a transformation of ts own and this is a must-have for this model to work successfully

- **Innovation Accounting**
  - This model includes a continuous evaluation of the risk, value, growth and potential ROI for projects
  - It enables choosing critical metrics that measure what matters in terms of end-user product engagement, assumption-testing, product risk and perceived current value. All of these enable the development of a product or service better aligned to customer and market needs. It also sets singularity of focus on the product development objectives for all team members
  - Benefits of this model include improved corporate governance and continual evaluation of the value with a focus on the upsides and downsides of a potential project being evaluated for funding

Assessing DevOps

What is a DevOps Assessment?

Adopting DevOps practices is not an overnight process. DevOps transfomations can be multi-year transformation programs done incrementally and across the organization while continuously learning from our failures. All this makes it important for any organization to know whether the practices they are following are in alignment with the DevOps initiative.

A DevOps Assesment is an assessment of different focus areas that are cornerstones to building a Devops organization. It consists of a set of questions that targeted stakeholders and focus groups from different organizational areas can answer and a holistic review of portfolios, key application workflows and enterprise architecture and culture. Based on the outcomes of this analysis, the organization can see whether it is moving in the right direction. A DevOps Assessment helps outline current awareness and adoption maturity of key practices and identify a road map of improvement areas.

Why do enterprises need a DevOps Assessment?

DevOps has transcended from being a buzzword to being a hot button item on the C-suite agenda today. More and more organizations are looking at rapidly transforming themselves leveraging DevOps.

While is is a proven fact that DevOps impacts the software devlopment processes, cycle time and delivery quality with an accelerated pace, it is equally true that it demands a lot of discipline to adopt newer ways of working. DevOps Assessment is real necessity to get an idea of where you are and where you can be on your DevOps journey.

Goal	How DevOps Assessment helps achieve?
Building a DevOps organization	• Helps you get a focused approach to understanding your readiness for DevOps or maturity with DevOps practices and align your sails to nurture a DevOps mindset • Helps you achieve clarity on the performance of different functional areas • Development and Operations teams to baseline their performance and know their strengths as well as areas of improvment • Talent acquisition team to have focused hiring of talent with DevOps mindset and skills • Management team to focus and target the key impact and investment areas • Infrastructure and Operations teams to identify the most business-critical operations
Increased organization wide collaboration	• Helps you identify siloed working anti-patterns that are detrimental to DevOps • Enables you to foster enhanced collaboration and transparency with practice like ChatOps • Enables the building of a high-performance culture
Increased agility	• Helps the organization to align its software devlopment and IT operations processes with strategic goals and reduce time to market without compromising on quality and reliability • Enables the organization to harness any change to the maimum benefit of the customer and deliver greater value

Goal	How DevOps Assessment helps achieve?
Efficient Release Management	• Helps you evaluate how your organization is currently using DevOps practices to support planning throughout the software development and release process • Scoring against practices that are critical to a DevOps culture helps you apprecuiate the gaps and bridge them with targeted solutions
Better Security and Lower Risk	• Helps establish the gaps and actions needed to achieve more stable, scalable and secure environments • Enhanced security means lower risks, improved compliance and no security breaches, losses and penalties therewith
Innovation	• More and more automated workflows, reduced number of incidents and defects and improved production stability makes time available to the team to explore more innovative solutions

What to ask prior to starting an Enterprise DevOps Assessment?

An organization with continuously changing technology and business landscape might be thinking of embarking or may have already e barked upon a DevOps initiative. It's important to ask the following questions at the start of a DevOps Assessment to understand the organization and its align with its strategic priorities and expectations.

It may be worthwhile to understand what benefits the leadership expects from an assessment and how are they going to approach the transformation overall. A clear understanding of these perspectives is crucial to establish a data-driven DevOps Transformation Strategy.

1. *What is your vision for change as an enterprise?*
2. *What are your strategic goals and objectives and how is DevOps aligned with helping you meet them?*
3. *Is your top management and executive layer supportive of and committed to the organizational vision for change?*
4. *Is your infrastructure and technology landscape flexible enough to embrace the recommendations from a full-fledged assessment involving rearchitecting the organizational systems or re-platforming existing applications?*
5. *Are there any programs running in the organization for enterprise portfolio modernization from monolith legacy applications to microservices?*
6. *Are you as an organization aspiring to move or have moved to virtualized services with multi-cloud deployments?*
7. *What benefits and business value do you anticipate from transforming your business with DevOps?*
8. *Does your existing organizational structure facilitate collaboration and sharing of tools between Dev, Ops and Infrastructure groups?*
9. *Does your organizational culture foster a "Product Mindset"?*
10. *Have you as an organization assessed your readiness for DevOps earlier?*
11. *What are your current mechanisms for performance assessments, reward and recognition?*
12. *Is your organization culture supportive of moving to role-based teams with a flat structure compared to a multi-tiered hierarchical structure?*
13. *How are projects and products prioritized and funded in your organization?*
14. *Which portfolios or business segments are your priority to transform as an organization?*

Milestones of a DevOps Assessment

An Enterprise DevOps Assessment is typically comprised of the following milestones, namely: Exploration, Discovery, Analysis and Retrospection and Collaboration. These are executed in a cyclic or iterative manner with continuous feedback.

Key activities in each of these milestones are illustrated in the following figure.

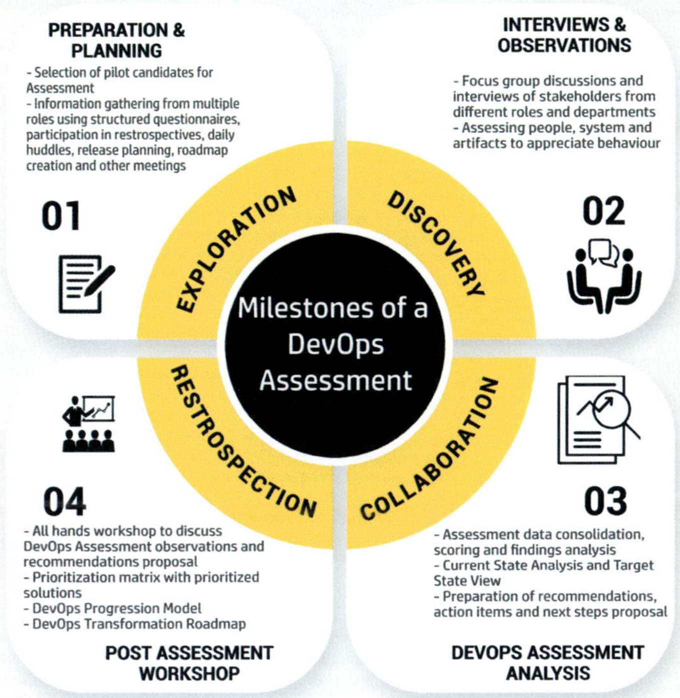

How long does it take for a DevOps Assessment?

A DevOps Assessment schedule will vary from organization to organization based on the scale of the portfolio or lines of business to be assessed and scope of technical practices in focus along with commonly applicable practices and key focus areas to be assessed.

A typical assessment for an organization of scale of around 500-700 people will vary anywhere between 4 to 6 weeks excluding training of people on pilot projects to be assessed with one enterprise DevOps coach and two additional DevOps technologists. These projects may then be taken up for implementation or replaced by alternate candidates for DevOps implementation based on Assessment outcomes.

A Sample DevOps Assessment Schedule is shown in the following figure.

Milestone	Timeline	Key Activities	Key Deliverables
Exploration	Week 1	• Understand Organzational Vision for Change, Strategic Objectives, Goals and their alignment to DevOps to address the goals • Understand the Governance structure for DevOps transformation. • Define criteria to select a project for assessment: Business criticality, Team size, Team composition, Technology stack, Release duration • Identify SMEs for both DevOps: Business, IT, Key Stakeholders • Identify relevant tools, existing technology documents for projects selected for assessments for DevOps and start review • Access to pilot applications and CI CD pipeline (JIRA, Jenkins, Artifactory, Maven, etc.) for DevOps transformation • Preparation of project plan for DevOps transformation • Conduct focus interview with key stakeholders and collect information on DevOps process and practices.	• Pilot Application selection criteria for DevOps • List of projects to be assessed and key stakeholders • Transformation Project Plan for DevOps transformation • Identification of framework of choice based on business context and strategic priorities for DevOps Transformation • Risks and mitigations/ workarounds identified for DevOps Transformation
Discovery	Week 2	• Kick-off discussions with identified projects for DevOps maturity assessment • Review of existing DevOps process documentation • Access to identified projects and project management systems (e.g. JIRA, Confluence, ServiceNow, Artifactory, Jenkins, etc.) for DevOps • Review available CI CD Process in selected projects for DevOps • Automation and Tools analysis for DevOps transformation	• Kick-off meeting notes with projects identified for assessment for DevOps transformation • Choice of framework for identified projects for agile transformation • Risks and mitigations/ workarounds identified for DevOps transformation • DevOps Assessment Progress Report • Stakeholder Interview notes
Discovery	Week 3	• Assessment of identified projects plus reporting; Ceremonies, Artifacts, Project level metrics, analyzing team agility and assessment • Analyze gaps between current state and future state for DevOps Transformation and conduct further interviews with stakeholders, if needed	• DevOps Assessment Progress Report • Stakeholders interview notes documents and analysis of gaps for DevOps transformation

Milestone	Timeline	Key Activities	Key Deliverables
Analysis and Retrospection	Week 4	• Prepare initial draft of Current State Assessment report for DevOps transformations • Refinement of Current State Assessment Report for DevOps transformation • Stakeholder all-hands meeting to discuss Action items and Recommendations in terms of People, Process, Tools and Automation for DevOps transformation. • High-Level Effort Estimate for Recommendations • Preparation of Prioritization Matrix for action items with timeline and ownership • Review the gap analysis done for DevOps transformation and plan for further assessment, if needed • Assess the current mature state for DevOps practices, processes and tools: Planning & Process, Source Control, Develop & Test, Build & Release, Deploy, Monitoring, Control/Measure	• Current State (As-Is) Assessment Report with maturity level in each practice area for DevOps transformation • Prioritization matrix with action items, effort estimate and ownership for DevOps Transformation • Assessment Progress Report for DevOps Transformation • DevOps Tools and automation (CI process) review report
Analysis and Retrospection	Week 5	• Identification of Skill gaps and training needed for DevOps transformation • Identify list of people to be trained and skills on which they need to be trained. Identify applications to start DevOps transformation. • Preparation of Training Plan (including role wise skills, estimation in hours and cost) • Initial draft of Target State Assessment Report	• Training Plan, including people and skills identification based on the gap analysis done and budgeting for DevOps Transformation • Target State Report for DevOps Transformation • Assessment Progress Report for DevOps Transformation • Proposed Tools and CI CD Pipeline for selected projects • Recommended DevOps Practices and tools • Recommended DevOps Metrics • DevOps Transformation roadmap
Collaboration	Week 6	• Refinement of Target State Report • Final Gap analysis for current DevOps practices based on - discussions with stakeholders, existing CI-CD pipeline process, interview notes • Finalizing on Recommendations and review based on - potential future state for DevOps practices, DevOps Transformation Roadmap, Metrics	• Assessment Progress Report for DevOps Transformation • Proposed Tools and CI-CD pipeline for selected projects • Recommended DevOps Practices and tools • Recommended DevOps Metrics • DevOps Transformation roadmap

What is the support needed from the Assessee Organization for a DevOps Assessment?

- Timely availability and active participation of stakeholders in interviews and audit conversations
- An understanding of key business priorities and challenges and business expectations from DevOps as an enabler to meet this
- An understanding of business and technology landscape to understand the overall scheme of applications and their business criticality
- Access to project/program locations (both physical and soft access)
- Access to CI-CD pipeline, SharePoint and other tools for project, service and pipeline management (JIRA, Confluence, ServiceNow, Jenkins, Docker, Kubernetes, etc.)
- Access to identified project/application documentation, reports, dashboards, BI Tools, end-user experience touchpoints, etc

Manpower / Skills needed for conducting a DevOps Assessment

Typically, you will need an Enterprise DevOps Coach and two DevOps Technologists or SMEs to assess an organization of a size of about 500-700 people in 6 weeks. A representative sample of SMEs from business, IT and operations including representatives from the projects identified for assessment will get assessed.

Typical skills and competencies for the DevOps Assessors are articulated in the following table.

Role	Example Competencies Needed
Enterprise DevOps Coach	• Should have a sound understanding of DevOps culture and appreciation of cultural differences when it comes to implementing DevOps with distributed teams • Must have experience in consulting and advising customers on business transformation and build services • Should have implementation of DevOps toolchain automation using tools like GitHub, Jenkins, Kubernetes, Docker, Chef, Junit, Selenium and Nagios • Must have implementation experience with Agile, Scrum, TDD and DevOps practices like CI, CD, Continuous Testing and Continuous Deployment • Must have experience in Cloud Services, Agile Practices and Transformation • Must have experience in multiple delivery strategies for DevOps (A/B deployment or blue/green deployment, canary deployments, rollback/rollforward strategy) • Must have experience in cloud assessment and migration strategies • Should have experience in cloud bursting and security paradigms
DevOps Technologist	• Must have experience in building continuous integration infrastructure, deployment pipelines, maintaining Artifactory repositories, creating highly available, scalable and robust production environment by using different delivery strategies • Should possess in-depth knowledge and project execution capabilities across various methodologies Including Agile, Scrum, etc. • Must have experience in configuration and infrastructure management and various operations tasks in DevOps stack • Good to have experience in providing support for highly critical banking applications and troubleshooting high-impact issues in real time • Should be able to create nightly build plan, release version artifacts, deploy into higher environments, automate unit testing, Veracode code scan • Should possess the ability to define high-level strategy for operations monitoring and risk mitigation • Should have good knowledge on Ansible/Chef/Puppet playbooks for multienvironment deployments

Outcomes of a DevOps Assessment

A DevOps Assessment provides a practical analysis of your organization's fundamental DevOps capabilities, with specific focus on execution practices that can help improve your software delivery velocity, collaboration and business impact.

How is a DevOps Assessment Structured?

A DevOps Assessment is a comprehensive analysis of how your organization operates with respect to what is necessitated from being a true DevOps organization. The outcomes provide clarity on the strategic goals you are seeking to establish as an organization keeping in mind your business context. It delivers a snapshot of your organization, helping you to determine the extent that you have embraced DevOps. Finally, it delivers a crisp, prioritized plan that defines the practical steps you should take to become more DevOps.

Thus said, a DevOps Assessment provides a comprehensive view of your organization's DevOps maturity and agility from the team to the enterprise level and is aimed to help you make practical recommendations while defining a DevOps enterprise transformation strategy.

Assessment Focus areas

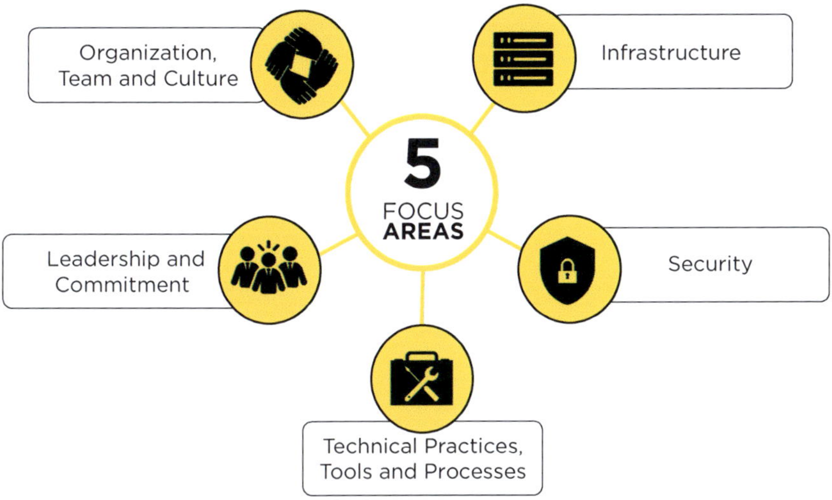

Selecting Pilot Candidates for Assessment

For all organizations embarking on the DevOps journey, selection of pilot candidates is crucial to their success. Candidates here may be projects, programs, products or portfolios. A successful pilot is one that acts as a proof of concept, creates lasting impact within the organization, making results visible and inspiring many more to onboard the train to transformation. Experiences required from DevOps adoption with the pilot can provide learnings and best practices that can be harnessed by other projects or applications for subsequent DevOps adoption.While many organizations choose to dive in head first without understanding the long and short of transformation, it may be worth the time and criticality to do a collective assessment on which candidates could generate a potential business impact and could be leveraged as DevOps ambassadors in the organization.

Some of the key points to remember while selecting candidates for the pilot are

- Start with a business need or a use-case to arrive at a potential list of candidate projects that can generate the desired impact.
- Be aggressive but start small and not big-bang to create a longlasting impact.

- The pilot project should be of a size that can easily be managed and will be successful in creating specific business value while getting all the attention it deserves.
- It may also be a good idea to blueprint the sprint wise plan for candidates selected and tackle not more than 3-4 specific practices of DevOps than going for an all practices implementation.

A successful pilot is critical for future growth and velocity of DevOps implementation in the organization. It should be rightly evangelized, popularized and the efforts should be messaged using appropriate communication canvas for maximizing the organizational impact. To select a pilot application, the following may be guiding criteria, although you will be governed by what is most applicable to your business context.

1. *What is the current release frequency for the application and will it benefit from shorter lead time to deployment?*
2. *Does the DevOps pilot for this application receive necessary leadership buy-in and support?*
3. *Is your application cross-departmental? In other words, does it have representation from multiple teams or organizational groups working together as a single team or it a single group heavily dependent on stakeholders from external groups?*
4. *Are the leaders or CIOs confident on the technology stack for the chosen application? Choice of an incorrect technology that doesn't address specific objectives can label a project as a failure in the absence of tech -savvy leadership evaluation.*
5. *Does the team in scope have a DevOps mindset with a willingness to embrace change and newer ways of working breaking silos as recommended by DevOps?*
6. *Can we look at DevOps adoption by the pilot application in scope within a short term like one quarter to showcase some quick wins?*
7. *Does the application use or is planning to use micro-services with loosely coupled or modular architectures?*
8. *Is the team size for this project adequate enough to achieve demonstrable impact? The size of the application team overall can be anywhere up to 100 people as well however these teams should be split into multiple development teams of a size of at about 10 to 15 for showcasing an impact.*
9. *What is the level of business, technical and financial risk associated with implementing DevOps in this application?*
10. *Is the application architecture continuously changing based on multiple and frequent demands for changes from the business and end users?*
11. *Does the application use tools that can be part of the overall enterprise DevOps toolchain?*
12. *What is the degree of automation currently implemented with this application?*

Assessment, Scope and Coverage

The assessment includes 8 DevOps disciplines and 3 dimensions People, Process and Technology broadly covered under 5 focus areas as illustrated in the following figure. Furthermore, each of these focus areas has multiple key practices each of which map to at least one of the DevOps disciplines and hence form the basis of assessment.

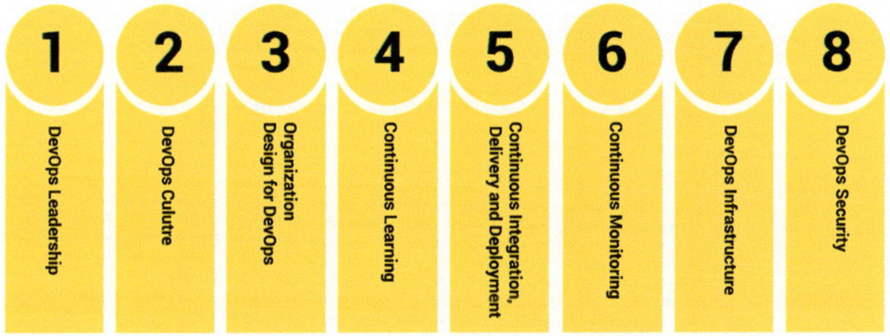

The 8 Disciplines of DevOps

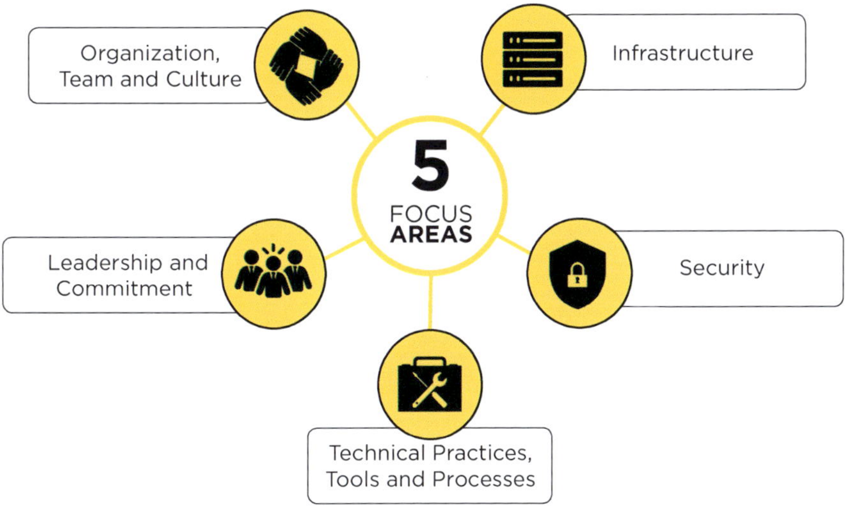

Within each of the 5 focus areas, there are multiple key practices that together define that focus area. Each of these key practices may map to 1 or more DevOps disciplines and has a focus group defined for assessment. DevOps scores are generated at a key practice level for respective teams.

The focus area and key practice composition is shown in the following figure

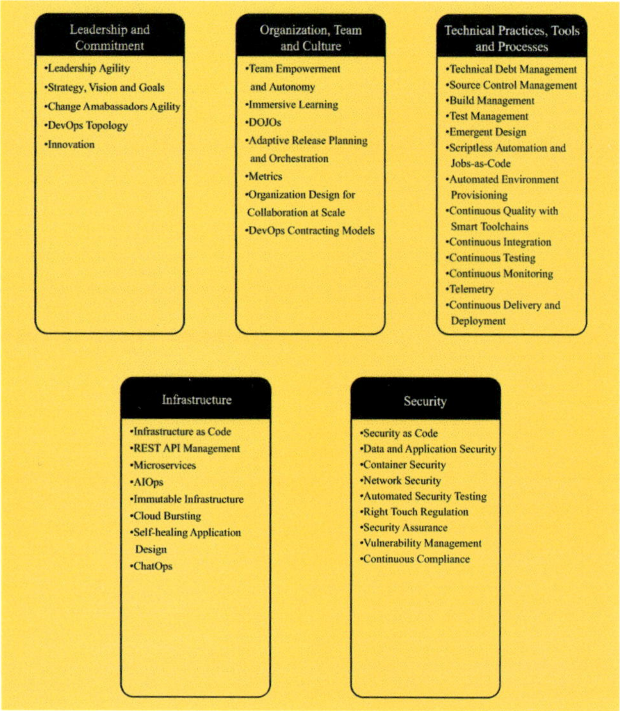

In the forthcoming pages, I have shared with you some of the questions from actual assessments that were conducted with numerous customers across domains globally. They may be further refined based on specific business context to be valuable aids for assessing enterprise readiness or maturity at a given point of time.

A DevOps Assessment is a comprehensive assessment that spans multiple such areas and examines current organizational behaviours, considering an organizational business context. Most leaders report high ROI from the assessment, as it steers their navigation on the road toward transformation

Focus Groups

The focus groups for these assessment conversations can be broadly bucketed under the following clusters. While Development and Operations teams define the core groups that will be evaluated for the technical practices that define a DevOps organization, all the other support groups are essential to influence change ingraining a DevOps mindset.

Focus Groups	Representative Sample
Executive Management	CIOs, Business Leaders, Managing Directors, Executive Directors, Directors, Vice Presidents and similar
Middle Management	Program Managers, Portfolio Managers, Product Owners, Project Managers and similar
Application Teams	Developers, Testers, Business Analysts, Solution Architects, Infrastructure and Operations representatives, Security specialists, SMEs from Business, IT and similar
Change Ambassadors	Agile and DevOps Coaches, Scrum Masters, Transformation Leads and similar
Business Enabling Functions	Human Resources, Legal, Procurement, Marketing and so on

Roles and titles may vary with different organizations. These are broad buckets.

Now that we have gone through everything around what an assessment is, why is it needed, how does it make a difference to the organization and what all is its scope of coverage, let's get into the actual assessment for each of these focus areas.

Collecting Assessment Data

As a CIO, I nominate 10 leaders and 20 application teams to be assessed based on my strategic priorities. How would the assessor assess and rate me? Here are some quick steps on this.

Action Item	Responsibility
Nominate candidates for assessment – leaders and pilot programs (includes applications)	CIO
Work with each leader on the applicability of key practices within each focus area for the pilot candidates	Assessor and Leaders
Arrive at the definition of Score of 1 to 5 for each key practice checkpoint (based on business organization and application context) where objectives scores are applicable	Assessor, Practitioners and Leaders
Have an all-hands session to bring all stakeholders together on the areas that will get assessed and the baselining of score definitions for each area	Assessor, Practitioners and Leaders
Walkthrough the Scoring Logic for each focus area (unless explicitly cited by CIO and Leadership, each focus area will carry an equal weightage of 20%). Score for each key practice will be an average of the scores for all checkpoints that are applicable. Subjective questions where scores are not applicable will be additionally helpful in crafting recommendations for the overall roadmap	Assessor
Walkthrough the expected Assessment Outcomes that will be in the form of an Assessment Recommendations Report. This will contain scores for each key practice and action items for the focus area overall. Set expectations on what to expect and what not to expect in an Assessment Recommendations Report	Assessor
List the Action Items Backlog and walk through each item with the respective focus group and leadership. Understand what it takes to takes to implement this action item in alignment with a prioritization done with the stakeholders based on effort involved and time to implement, potential savings and benefits achieved and alignment with strategic priorities	Assessors and Leaders
Craft a Transformation Roadmap based on a timeline and priority identifying the immediate, near-term and long-term actions	Assessors and Leaders

Part 2

Leadership & Commitment

Leadership & Commitment

Leadership and Commitment for Business Transformation

The success of any organizational level transformation is directly proportional to the degree of commitment and support from its leadership and top management. Thus said, it is sheerly this pillar that drives all others to make change happen.

Assessment Objectives

Assessing leadership and commitment enables establishing an objective view in terms of how the leaders drive change in the organization, lead and engage people effectively. It also aims to understand the effectiveness of change initiatives, all of which can enable a successful transformation or promote change fatigue.

Key Practices Summary

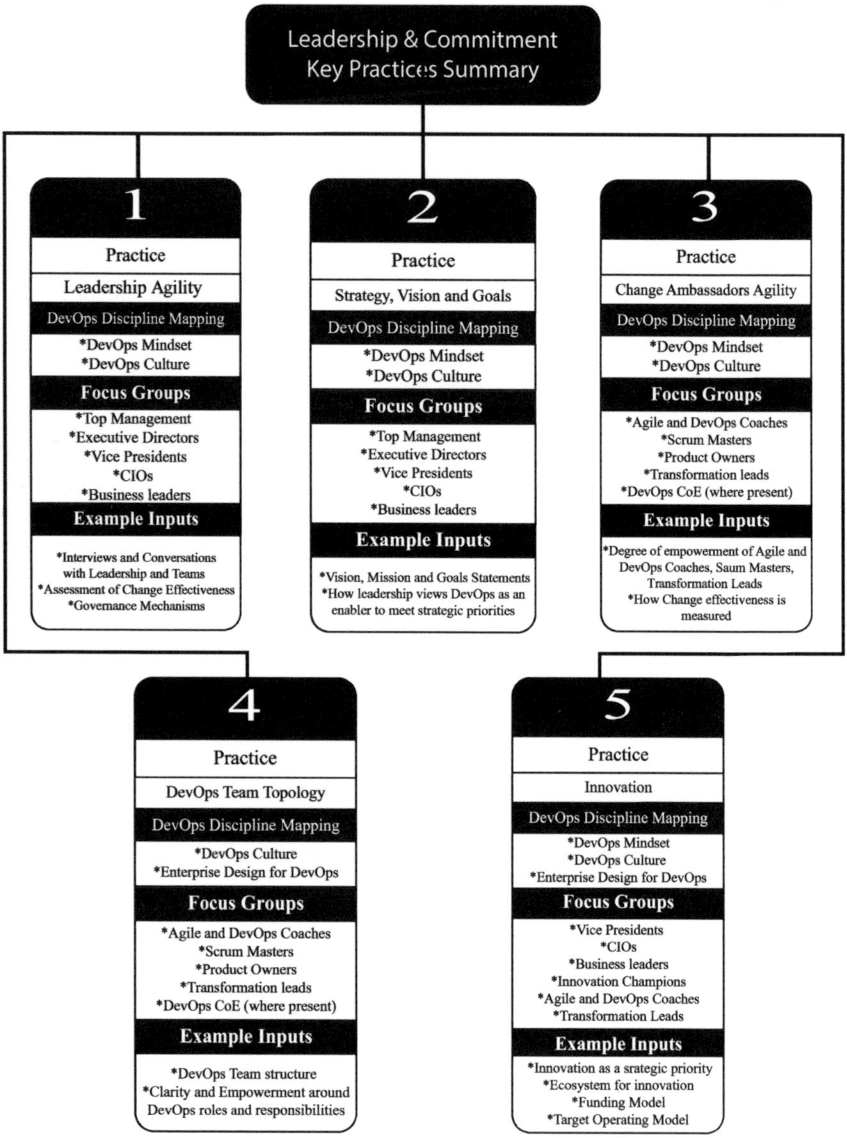

Leadership Agility

Leadership agility is the ability to make time-sensitive and effective decisions and actions in a volatile, complex and dynamically changing business landscape.

Why Assess?

The purpose of assessing leadership agility is to understand the strengths and limitations of leadership and organizational culture. The assessment questions are more of a diagnostic that focus not only on the culture but also on inter-group collaboration dynamics e.g., between the top management and the execution layer, between different CIO organizations as well as between different divisions of an organization.

Key Practice Summary

1

Practice

Leadership Agility

DevOps Discipline Mapping

*DevOps Mindset
*DevOps Culture

Focus Groups

*Top Management
*Executive Directors
*Vice Presidents
*CIOs
*Business leaders

Example Inputs

*Interviews and Conversations with Leadership and Teams
*Assessment of Change Effectiveness
*Governance Mechanisms

Assessment Questions

**Questions to be scored on a scale of 1 to 5 (5 being ideal)*

***OSNA implies Objective Score Not Applicable*

Question	Score
1. How proactive and adaptive are your processes when it comes to aligning with any change?	**OSNA
2. Do your processes have the capability to sense and signal early warnings and risks?	**OSNA
3. What is the degree of organizational readiness for change?	① ② ③ ④ ⑤
4. Are all channels/roles and forums being leveraged to communicate the right message to the organizational groups, key stakeholders and the right people in a timely fashion?	**OSNA
5. Are senior leaders, executive management, transformation champions and change agents exhibiting the growth mindset and walking the talk?	**OSNA
6. To what extent are change leadership coaching, connect forums and 360-degree feedback tools being applied to influence leadership Behaviour when needed to create a more open and collaborative culture aligned to DevOps?	① ② ③ ④ ⑤
7. To what extent does your leadership nurture a culture where leadership shares credit for team wins and accepts blame for all failures on a consistent and ongoing basis? Cite some example situations.	① ② ③ ④ ⑤
8. To what extent does your leadership create a common ecosystem along with shared vision and goals for DevOps that nurture diversity and inclusivity of thoughts and ideas across the organization. Cite some examples of such situations that have included multiple diverse viewpoints and influenced decision making.	① ② ③ ④ ⑤
9. To what extent does your leadership take the ownership of driving organizational change collaboratively? What are some of the tough decisions you have faced so far while embarking on your DevOps journey?	① ② ③ ④ ⑤
10. What are some of the challenges you see on the near horizon? And how do you plan to address them and drive organizational change effectively?	**OSNA
11. To what extent do you empower your teams to make rapid and successful decisions in a decentralized manner? Cite few instances illustrating the situation.	① ② ③ ④ ⑤
12. To what extent have impediments thrashed on an ongoing basis to quickly take away key roadblocks and hindrances while undergoing implementation? How do you ensure the effectiveness of this mechanism for all programs that are part of the transformation? Cite few examples illustrating this.	① ② ③ ④ ⑤

13.	To what extent does your leadership nurture reciprocal relationships with other leaders who are on the transformation journey? And how does this collectively influence the transformation success?	(1) (2) (3) (4) (5)
14.	What kind of relationships does your leadership nurture in the organization? To what extent do you see these as critical to transformation success with DevOps?	(1) (2) (3) (4) (5)
15.	What are the organizational behaviours will your leadership prioritize to influence for change?	**OSNA
16.	What are the top 3 metrics in your view that will measure the success of your leadership throughout the DevOps journey?	**OSNA
17.	How often has your leadership exhibited the servant leader behaviours for your teams / organization? Cite few examples illustrating this.	(1) (2) (3) (4) (5)
18.	To what extent is there a focus on grooming leadership to model the new ways of working as a key strategy to nurture the DevOps culture?	(1) (2) (3) (4) (5)

Leaders Think

A DevOps transformation can lead to an extensive change in mindset and culture within an organization. But the transformation itself cannot be possible without the right mindset and culture. Leaders must understand what 'DevOps' really means. They are responsible to ingrain a mindset within the teams that breaks the barriers of 'Change' v/s 'Stability', by helping them adopt the right practices. In the words of Edward Deming - "The job of a leader is to accomplish transformation of his organization. He possesses knowledge, personality, and persuasive power. What is in his own head is not enough. He must convince and change enough people in power to make it happen. He possesses persuasive power. He understands people." DevOps is all about breaking the silos within large set-ups - starting with the leaders.

Sanjeev Kulkarni, CEO and Founder, Productshaala

Strategy, Vision and Goals

The Vision of any organization is a goal. It is different from strategy; strategy is an execution tool that enables one to maintain or achieve the Vision. Understanding Strategy, Vision, Mission and Goals is critical in aligning your transformation efforts with DevOps.

Why Assess?

The purpose of assessing this area is to understand what the organizational perspectives and strategic priorities are and how these maps to DevOps are helping them transform the organization and business.

Key Practice Summary

2
Practice
Strategy, Vision and Goals
DevOps Discipline Mapping
*DevOps Mindset *DevOps Culture
Focus Groups
*Top Management *Executive Directors *Vice Presidents *CIOs *Business leaders
Example Inputs
*Vision, Mission and Goals Statements *How leadership views DevOps as an enabler to meet strategic priorities

Assessment Questions

**Questions to be scored on a scale of 1 to 5 (5 being ideal)*

***OSNA implies Objective Score Not Applicable*

Question	Score
1. What are the top 3 goals of the organization?	**OSNA
2. What are the top 3 pain points of the organization?	**OSNA
3. To what extent do you see DevOps support you to accomplish the top 3 strategic goals and pain points of your organization?	① ② ③ ④ ⑤
4. To what extent do your delivery processes align with your enterprise strategy and vision?	① ② ③ ④ ⑤
5. Are your organizational processes analyzed for trends and patterns and retrospected for continuous improvement on an ongoing basis?	**OSNA
6. To what extent do your processes have clearly published roles, responsibilities, accountabilities and empowerment for decision making with authorized individuals?	① ② ③ ④ ⑤
7. How well aligned are your processes to ensure superior customer experience?	① ② ③ ④ ⑤
8. To what extent are your customers and other stakeholders educated on Agile / DevOps and similar areas when you experience a gap in collaboration and engagement from the Customer on one such transformation?	① ② ③ ④ ⑤
9. To what extent are you cohesively identifying and nurturing a desired culture that supports the business strategy and change vision for DevOps?	① ② ③ ④ ⑤
10. To what extent are you actively and thoughtfully shifting underlying mindsets while alongside acquiring new capabilities?	① ② ③ ④ ⑤
11. To what extent are competencies and skills being regularly assessed and upgraded across the impacted organization?	① ② ③ ④ ⑤
12. To what extent are the organizational processes and workflow being assessed and refined to enable optimization and new ways of working?	① ② ③ ④ ⑤
13. What are your key selection criteria for hiring internal or external coaches, scrum masters and change agents for influencing change with DevOps?	**OSNA
14. To what extent are your hiring processes indicative of bringing in new talent that is aligned with your forward-thinking vision for the organization?	① ② ③ ④ ⑤

15. How do you ensure that your change champions possess a mix of different skill sets like those listed below and what are your strategies to constantly groom them? a. Behavioural specialists for influencing flow and change b. Technologists that facilitate an end-to-end DevOps toolchain c. Process specialists with application delivery and support backgrounds d. Business specialists with an understanding of agile and DevOps	**OSNA

Leaders Think

Successful adoption of DevOps requires strategic thinking, significant commitment from top management and a laser focus to make it successful. Unless the leaders are clear on how DevOps will help them address their pain areas or achieve their strategic goals, a DevOps transformation can never be successful. These drivers that create the vision and goals may be external or internal. Examples of external drivers include improving CSAT by meeting expectations around cycle time, reliability, usability, availability, performance, features, value and time to market. Examples of internal drivers include improving operational efficiency or improving employee engagement, improving technical competencies or simply making deployments more selfhealing.

Sonal Drone, Managing Consultant, IBM

Businesses today are extremely dynamic. In order for businesses to survive in today's highly competitive market they need to have a Leadership that helps create a competitive business advantage. What this means is bringing new, high quality services or products into the market at a rapid pace to address customers implicit and explicit needs and help solving their problems with a high level of satisfaction. When we talk about the IT industry, DevOps helps to bring in the much-needed agility in the development process to quickly deploy and integrate pieces of workable code to delight the customer leading to improved customer experience. However, experience shows it is easier said than done. Implementing DevOps is a change in mindset, culture and way of working and requires a high degree of transformational leadership to be in place to make the change happen. Organizations need to assess if they have the right leadership in place, a culture where mistakes are accepted and not penalized and empowered teams that accept failure and quickly learn from mistakes.

Embarking on the DevOps journey without doing a proper assessment on the prevailing organization environment is bound to be a disaster. As Leaders we need participate in the azssessment process to understand and communicate in a clear and transparent manner, across the organization the drivers leading to change, priorities that need to be in place, support available from leadership, roles and responsibilities, how teams will be formed and need to function and what is the outcome expected. In my opinion having the right Leadership is a single most important factor ensuring a successful transformation towards an Agile and efficient DevOps organization as it tightly integrates Software development and IT Operations to work together as one trusted collaborative team.

Vishwajeet Jathar, Founder, Winspire Learnings

Change Ambassadors Agility

An organization's change agility is the agility with which it responds to both external drivers of change to stay competitive as well as proactively harness change to drive continuous improvement internally. It is here that change ambassadors agility comes in being empowering change ambassadors appropriate to take the right decisions with an agile mindset and work with people towards transformation goals.

Why Assess?

- Enables empowerment of change agents to influence teams embrace to the DevOps mindset
- Enables change ambassadors to propagate and demonstrate the right set of key practices that will foster DevOps adoption in teams.

Key Practice Summary

Assessment Questions

**Questions to be scored on a scale of 1 to 5 (5 being ideal)*

***OSNA implies Objective Score Not Applicable*

Question	Score
1. To what extent are your change management strategies effective? How do you lead and motivate a team through change?	① ② ③ ④ ⑤
2. To what extent are leaders leveraging the positivity and motivation created by quick-term wins to address bigger problems?	① ② ③ ④ ⑤
3. To what extent is there an urgency to transform throughout the enterprise?	① ② ③ ④ ⑤
4. To what extent is there a dedicated sponsor for the change effort along with governance being established to oversee and refine execution of the transformation roadmap and to maintain the momentum to transform?	① ② ③ ④ ⑤
5. To what extent is the effort inclusive of multiple influential leaders throughout the organization?	① ② ③ ④ ⑤
6. To what extent do you see each change initiative as part of the total transformation, having daily leadership positioned to organize the program's multiple work streams, take charge of the roadmap, identify necessities, dispel barriers and further execution of tasks?	① ② ③ ④ ⑤
7. To what extent is there an internal sufficiency of talent with the right skills and mindsets dedicated to support the change effort?	① ② ③ ④ ⑤
8. To what extent have key stakeholders who are critical to transformation success been identified and their core value drivers been understood?	① ② ③ ④ ⑤
9. To what extent is it understood the ways in which stakeholders will be proactive in leading the change over a period of time, building their support for the transformation?	① ② ③ ④ ⑤
10. To what extent has a cadre of top change agents been identified and rallied for active involvement across all aspects of discussing transformation milestones?	① ② ③ ④ ⑤
11. To what extent is this set of early adopters of change treated like a pioneering group of change agents and ambassadors of change?	① ② ③ ④ ⑤
12. To what extent are both internal and external change agents empowered to influence change in the team?	① ② ③ ④ ⑤

Leaders Think

Building a true DevOps organization requires strong champions of change who will advocate and influence the traditional ways of working. Change Agents must be empowered to drive change in their respective portfolios and enable teams to visualize how DevOps will help them meet their strategic goals. The success of a DevOps initiative is directly proportional to its Change Ambassadors Agility.

Umesh Jain, Vice President, Deutsche Bank Group

Change Ambassadors play a critical role in ensuring that the full benefits of Agility are achieved not just by changing processes, ways of working but also leveraging the benefits of DevOps. Usually it has been observed that there is less focus on DevOps and more on the process side of the things. DevOps transformation (be it full CI/CD, branching/merging strategy or efficiency through tools) has to be on the equal priority if not higher on the Change Ambassadors Agility backlog. Many process level initiatives undertaken do not reap full benefits in the absence of any parallel such initiatives in the DevOps area.

Ashutosh Bhatawadekar, Enterprise Agile Consultant, Tata Consultancy Services

DevOps Team Topology

The DevOps Topologies is a collection of patterns that illustrates team structures and practices together, all of which influence the success of DevOps adoption and transformation.

Why Assess?

The purpose of assessing this area is to understand DevOps transformation is being driven and perceived across the organization. If there is a DevOps Center of Excellence (CoE) and all the project teams think that DevOps Transformation is the job of the CoE, then they are set to fail. Contrary to this, if the projects themselves have teams that are self-sufficient to execute DevOps, they may be more motivated and sustainable. Assessing this area thus helps to get this view in assessing projects.

Key Practice Summary

4
Practice
DevOps Team Topology
DevOps Discipline Mapping
*DevOps Culture *Enterprise Design for DevOps
Focus Groups
*Agile and DevOps Coaches *Scrum Masters *Product Owners *Transformation leads *DevOps CoE (where present)
Example Inputs
*DevOps Team structure *Clarity and Empowerment around DevOps roles and responsibilities

Assessment Questions

**Questions to be scored on a scale of 1 to 5 (5 being ideal)*

***OSNA implies Objective Score Not Applicable*

Question	Score
1. To what extent are QA testers integrated into the CI-CD cycle?	① ② ③ ④ ⑤
2. To what extent does your DevOps team have a multidisciplinary and cross-functional skill set?	① ② ③ ④ ⑤
3. To what extent is DevOps a collective responsibility of all programs and projects in the organization?	① ② ③ ④ ⑤
4. To what extent is Ops an integral part of the DevOps Team and does it participate in all decisions pertaining to the project including overall deployment or migration strategies? Is Ops invited to the project kickoff? When does involvement of Ops start in the overall project lifecycle?	① ② ③ ④ ⑤
5. To what extent are Security specialists involved in the project life cycle? Are they invited to kickoffs? What is their role in technical decision making?	① ② ③ ④ ⑤
6. To what extent are your DevOps teams organized around value streams to deliver business value for a given customer segment?	① ② ③ ④ ⑤
7. To what extent are there interdependencies and challenges when multiple teams collaborate to achieve the aforesaid goal?	① ② ③ ④ ⑤
8. To what extent does your DevOps team enable visibility of work and flow?	① ② ③ ④ ⑤
9. Does this also include the visibility of defects, risks, technical debt and spikes in addition to stories that deliver business value?	**OSNA
10. To what extent does your DevOps team measure the time it takes from code commit to deployment? How are the results identified for bottlenecks?	① ② ③ ④ ⑤
11. To what extent do your teams practice inner-sourcing or similar practices that facilitate parallel development through codebases while also ensuring integrity of the code?	① ② ③ ④ ⑤

Leaders Think

For a DevOps transformation, it must be a collective dream of the organization championed by every single member of the portfolio where DevOps. A CoE can facilitate conversations or support the cause but it cannot own or drive DevOps across the organization. Thus said, a CoE for DevOps can be an enabler for helping teams succeed with DevOps. Focus on embracing the multiple roles with DevOps and adopting DevOps ways of working will go a long way in transforming the organization culture.

Umesh Jain, Vice President, Deutsche Bank Group

Change Ambassadors play a critical role in ensuring that the full benefits of Agility are achieved not just by changing processes, ways of working but also leveraging the benefits of DevOps. Usually it has been observed that there is less focus on DevOps and more on the process side of the things. DevOps transformation (be it Full CI/CD, Branching/Merging strategy or efficiency through tools) has to be on the equal priority if not higher on the Change Ambassadors Agility backlog. Many process level initiatives undertaken do not reap full benefits in the absence of any parallel such initiatives in the DevOps area.

Ashutosh Bhatawadekar, Enterprise Agile Consultant, Tata Consultancy Services

Innovation

Innovation is a practice that involves multiple techniques to uncover new ways to do things. Innovations apply for management and organizations on all layers, sizes, across segments and operating in all industries.

Why Assess?

The purpose of assessing this area is to understand competitive edge, business differentiation, market footprint and leadership and eventually, higher profitability and revenue.

Key Practice Summary

5

Practice

Innovation

DevOps Discipline Mapping

*DevOps Mindset
*DevOps Culture
*Enterprise Design for DevOps

Focus Groups

*Vice Presidents
*CIOs
*Business leaders
*Innovation Champions
*Agile and DevOps Coaches
*Transformation Leads

Example Inputs

*Innovation as a srategic priority
*Ecosystem for innovation
*Funding Model
*Target Operating Model

Assessment Questions

**Questions to be scored on a scale of 1 to 5 (5 being ideal)*

***OSNA implies Objective Score Not Applicable*

Question		Score
1.	To what extent do you treat innovation-led growth as key to organization growth?	1 2 3 4 5
2.	Do your vision, mission and strategic goals reflect the criticality of innovation-led growth?	**OSNA
3.	To what extent are your targets for innovation effectively cascaded through the organization layers till teams?	1 2 3 4 5
4.	To what extent are your people motivated, recognized, rewarded and organized to innovate continuously?	1 2 3 4 5
5.	To what extent does your organization foster an ecosystem to experiment, fail, learn and innovate?	1 2 3 4 5
6.	To what extent do you reinforce the culture of innovation parenting and open organizational space to innovators to let the creativity flow in without barriers?	1 2 3 4 5
7.	To what extent do you encourage outside-in and system thinking in your product ideation stage and all through the life cycle?	1 2 3 4 5
8.	To what extent are transformation outcomes influencing digital transformation?	1 2 3 4 5
9.	To what extent are major business initiatives engineered to role model and reinforce the desired innovation culture?	1 2 3 4 5
10.	To what extent are major business initiatives engineered to role model and reinforce the desired innovation culture?	1 2 3 4 5
11.	To what extent does your organization foster a culture of connectors and multipliers that lead by example?	1 2 3 4 5
12.	To what extent does your organization and team factor innovation as a part of the overall organization strategy?	1 2 3 4 5
13.	To what extent is innovation promoted as part of the organizational behaviour?	1 2 3 4 5
14.	To what extent will the underlying technology, infrastructure and toolsuite support value creation through and customer-oriented productive processes?	1 2 3 4 5
15.	To what extent is it possible to lead in technological innovation and predict the needs and experiences of the future while also focusing on positive social impact?	1 2 3 4 5
16.	To what extent is DevOps instrumental in achieving this goal?	1 2 3 4 5

Leaders Think

In my opinion Innovation cuts across departmental boundaries and is a highly cross-functional process. Many times though the foundation for innovation is technology based the competence required to take through innovations requires many other skills and goes beyond technical competence. Since innovative solutions arise from complex interactions between many stakeholders organizations and environmental factors implementing DevOps can have a synergistic effect for driving innovation across organizations and help transform products and services into integrated value driven solutions keeping the end customer in mind. You can actually accelerate innovation with DevOps where new ideas can be translated into solutions and continuously integrated and improved. Coupled with Design Thinking you can really take your innovation process to a new level.

Design Thinking will help you come closer to the customer and think on creating customer centric solutions and DevOps will help you to deploy the solutions faster to the market with high quality taking the whole customer experience to a new level. In my opinion if we look at the innovation process then Design Thinking is where the birth of a new idea for a problem takes place and DevOps is where the idea can be quickly translated into a deployable solution. Companies should strongly think about combining Design Thinking principles along with implementing DevOps to cut across silo's, improve collaboration and communication across teams and stakeholders in order to stay ahead of competition.

Vishwajeet Jathar, Founder, Winspire Learnings

Organization, Team & Culture

Organization, Team & Culture

Organization Design and its influence on Business Transformation

When we assess organizational culture, most managers, teams and leaders presume they have already embraced agile and DevOps. The fact remains they have not. Probably a couple of product development teams have adopted a few engineering practices, which is not analogous with influencing the organization to be ready for DevOps. Such is the influence of organizational design on business transformation. Merely copying structures will not replicate the desired shift in culture.

In a VUCA world of today where decisions are made overnight and customers are not willing to wait for long to realize their ambitious products, it is important that all the components of an organization are ready for the change. All the parts of the organization resonate with what it takes to achieve a successful DevOps transformation. This includes the human resources, finance, legal and contracting teams as well to work in alignment with redesigning for a DevOps organization.

Assessment Objectives

Some of the key objectives in assessing this area include but are not limited to the following.

- Understanding organizational behaviour requires understanding leadership and team behaviours
- Organizational culture grows from its grassroots and across. Thus said, culture varies with teams, regions, business units and leadership. Hence, it is important to assess how decisions are made, how autonomy is granted to people, how leadership is the binding glue for the organization, all of which define the organization and team culture

Key Practices Summary

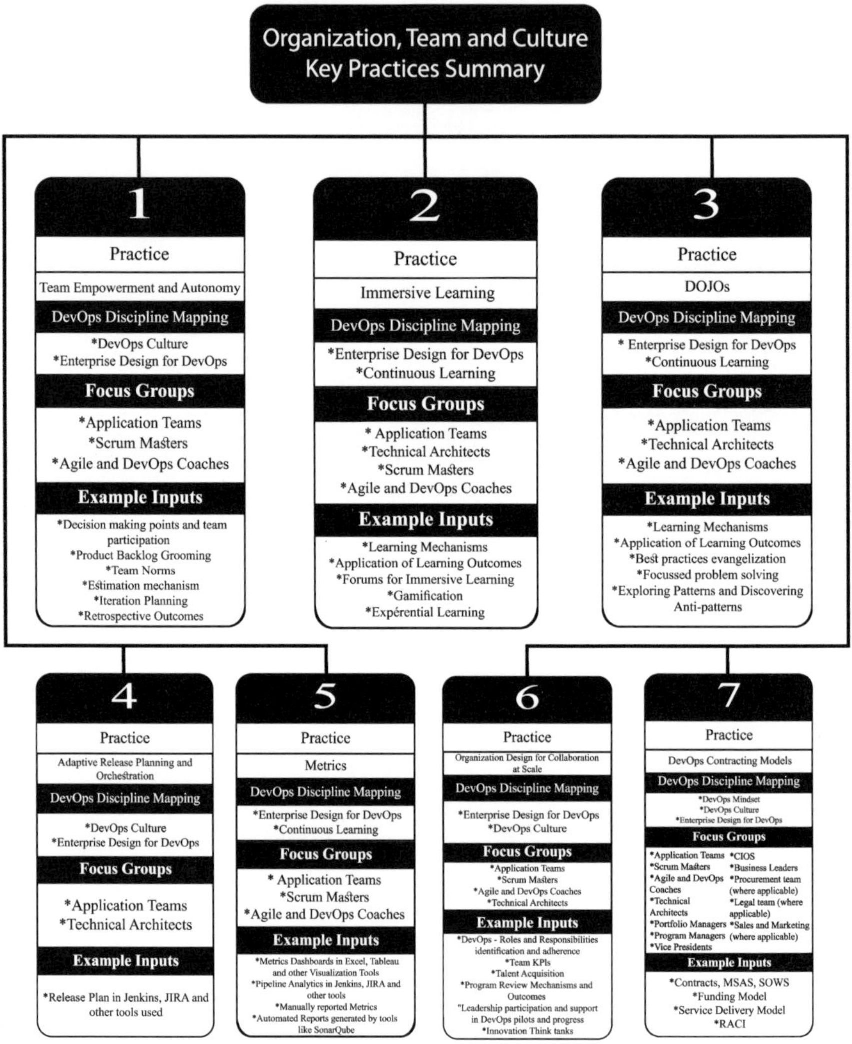

Team Empowerment and Autonomy

Team empowerment and autonomy is a key practice that drives teams to become self-sufficient and enables decentralized decision making in the best interests of a team collaboratively with specific goals. This is a critical success factor for ingraining high performance in any organization.

Why Assess?

Employees who feel empowered in their roles are more engaged, make better decisions, remain self-motivated and deliver a quality product that enables an organization to remain nimble and productive which in these times is necessary for survival. An organization structured around empowered teams will gravitate towards a flat hierarchy and wide spectrum of highly passionate and trusted human assets. Hence team empowerment and autonomy become an increasingly important assessment area in the scheme of operations for DevOps.

Key Practice Summary

1
Practice
Team Empowerment and Autonomy
DevOps Discipline Mapping
*DevOps Culture *Enterprise Design for DevOps
Focus Groups
*Application Teams *Scrum Masters *Agile and DevOps Coaches
Example Inputs
*Decision making points and team participation *Product Backlog Grooming *Team Norms *Estimation mechanism *Iteration Planning *Retrospective Outcomes

Assessment Questions

**Questions to be scored on a scale of 1 to 5 (5 being ideal)*

***OSNA implies Objective Score Not Applicable*

Question		Score
1.	To what extent do your workspaces promote osmotic communication?	(1) (2) (3) (4) (5)
2.	To what extent are those doing the actual work deciding the actual estimates together with the Product Owner?	(1) (2) (3) (4) (5)
3.	To what extent does the team pull tasks based on what is done and what they can do next or are the work allocations per resource done centrally by the Project Manager or Scrum Master?	(1) (2) (3) (4) (5)
4.	To what extent does management keep the scope stable and unchanged in between an ongoing iteration?	(1) (2) (3) (4) (5)
5.	To what extent does such a reprioritization also descope an equivalent amount of work from the iteration?	(1) (2) (3) (4) (5)
6.	To what extent is capacity planning of the team a collective exercise?	(1) (2) (3) (4) (5)
7.	When someone in your team takes a planned or an unplanned off, how is capacity planning done with the existing team?	**OSNA
8.	In case of an emergency leave by a team member, how are others in the team able to manage the deliveries?	**OSNA
9.	To what extent is your team self-sufficient in terms of all the skills needed for delivery execution?	(1) (2) (3) (4) (5)
10.	Does your team encourage the Specialist or Generalist culture?	**OSNA
11.	Are specialists willing to work on areas outside their core areas of expertise in the interest of the team?	**OSNA
12.	To what extent are retrospectives and system demos leveraged from a feedback and continual improvement perspective?	(1) (2) (3) (4) (5)
13.	To what extent is the team comfortable in harnessing change to the customer's advantage?	(1) (2) (3) (4) (5)
14.	To what extent does the team see the MVP as their common goal to achieve or is each member working on his/her individual KPIs, e.g., number of user stories delivered to testing, number of bugs per user story and so on?	(1) (2) (3) (4) (5)
15.	To what extent does the team celebrate collective wins or react to failures?	(1) (2) (3) (4) (5)
16.	To what extent is there a clear set of norms defined and being adhered to?	(1) (2) (3) (4) (5)

Leaders Think

The conventional organizational set-up organizations rewarded, the authoritative layer of leaders, for pushing teams and making decisions, for faster deliveries. As the organizations move to DevOps transformation, they have to be mindful of the fact that, the leaders may some unlearning to do. Additionally, in the traditional organizational environments, leaders may have unintentionally caused atrophy, in their teams as earlier, leaders thought thru the complexities, dependencies and took a lot of decisions, as a result of which there will be lots of skills and competencies that the team never developed since they were not directly exposed to such learning opportunities. There will be a significant change in the leaders' responsibilities, one of which is to impart those skills to the team to help them embark on the journey of self-organizing. Here's where leader's elasticity and willingness to take up a totally different role and acceptance of shifting to the background from forefront is crucial to this journey.

The organizations should invest in assessing and benchmarking the readiness of their leaders to fit into the skin of a "servant leader". Competency analysis and professional coaching have some proven methods to create that support structure for the leaders, as, they are the "Key Change Agents" in the transformation journey. Just the way leaders must UNLEARN, so must the teams. The teams do want empowerment, but empowerment along with responsibility is the complete package they signup for. In order to take well informed decisions that the teams can stand-by, even the teams have to be up-skilled to sense, observe & assess all aspects at greater depths. Team's readiness for being open to being vulnerable and collaborative must be assessed. Similar kind of support structure of coaching key influencers in the team, will reduce the friction during the DevOps journey. Finally, the organizations must stop rewarding the leaders for "pushing their teams" and also the teams for "being obedient followers and delivering on time". The organization must shift focus on team's professional progression & growth. The traditional known zone of the techno-functional skills alone, without any cognitive and social skills will not make the leaders "servants" nor will it make the teams "self-organizing".

Prachi Saraph, Director – Engineering, Guavus Network Systems

Immersive Learning

Immersive learning is a key practice of leveraging learning in simulated or artificial environments while retaining effectiveness for the learner. It skillfully combines the best of digital worlds using simulators, learning games and complex digital media with connected online learning environments, chat rooms and classrooms.

Why Assess?

- Immersive Environments (IEs) facilitate deeper learning of competencies relevant for success in today's connected world
- Increases learnability as it simulates real-life examples for the learner and generates personalized areas of improvement
- Enables assessments of the targeted competencies in a virtual environment with no proctoring

Key Practice Summary

2

Practice

Immersive Learning

DevOps Discipline Mapping

*Enterprise Design for DevOps
*Continuous Learning

Focus Groups

* Application Teams
*Technical Architects
*Scrum Masters
*Agile and DevOps Coaches

Example Inputs

*Learning Mechanisms
*Application of Learning Outcomes
*Forums for Immersive Learning
*Gamifcation
*Expérential Learning

Assessment Questions

**Questions to be scored on a scale of 1 to 5 (5 being ideal)*

***OSNA implies Objective Score Not Applicable*

Question		Score
1.	To what extent are various forums and mechanisms available in the organization for learning new technologies?	① ② ③ ④ ⑤
2.	To what extent is learning rewarded or promoted as part of the overall organizational strategy?	① ② ③ ④ ⑤
3.	To what extent is learning made mandatory as a part of every employee's learning goals?	① ② ③ ④ ⑤
4.	To what extent does your learning culture get reflected in your talent acquisition and nurturing strategy?	① ② ③ ④ ⑤
5.	To what extent are there avenues for constructive feedback that feed hungry minds to acquire and proliferate more and more knowledge?	① ② ③ ④ ⑤
6.	To what extent is gamification leveraged to address any of the strategic objectives for learning?	① ② ③ ④ ⑤
7.	To what extent do you drive effective engagement through learning programs?	① ② ③ ④ ⑤
8.	To what extent is time actively budgeted for dedicated Learning and Development?	① ② ③ ④ ⑤
9.	To what extent is knowledge-sharing part of the organizational culture?	① ② ③ ④ ⑤
10.	To what extent are there avenues and open channels to share learning acquired from failures?	① ② ③ ④ ⑤
11.	To what extent are learnings acquired from failures celebrated and rewarded?	① ② ③ ④ ⑤
12.	To what extent does leadership nurture and groom young talent that exhibit extraordinary learning skills?	① ② ③ ④ ⑤
13.	To what extent does leadership define and exhibit behaviours that unlock the focus towards learning?	① ② ③ ④ ⑤

Leaders Think

Softskills and Culture play an important part in developing high performing DevOps teams. Business simulation games are forms of 'experiential learning' in which end-to-end stakeholders can be brought together to learn. Not only will they learn to apply DevOps practices, such as the 3 ways, visualization, retrospectives but more importantly they will develop 'communication', 'collaboration' and 'continual learning & improvement' skills. Multiple surveys conducted globally have also revealed that 'collaboration' is a top scoring needed softskill. A business simulation can also form part of a DOJO, at the end of the simulation teams capture a list of concrete, pragmatics takeaways that can be input into the DOJO, allowing the teams to further experiment and explore these newly discovered behaviours.

Paul Wilkinson, Founder & CEO, GamingWorks

Immersive learning had been one of my personal experiences in the recent times when culture of MOOC started revolutionizing how individuals learn and how MOOC offered plethora of systematic learning choices to many who do not have luxury to enter into full time education being employed full time. Right from a course on "Machine Learning" to "Teaching Character and Creating Positive Classrooms", I have personally soaked myself in the sea of knowledge available on online MOOC platforms such as Coursera, Udemy and many others.

Albeit the fact that we have world class professors from top notch universities in the world, who have generated immersive learning contents in areas of their subject expertise with very creative audio and visual contents, we do not see many organizations utilizing these platforms and promoting it internally for organizational learning and development. DevOps is not just a concept but a culture which must be embraced fully to improve company's overall throughput. DevOps is much more than learning a programming language and immersive learning culture not just for DevOps but in every aspect of employee development would unleash, in a true sense, the power of human and organizational development.

Akhil Bhansali, Founder & CEO, Agile Beings

We often find it challenging to free employees for training due to tight delivery schedules, frequent modification, lack of sufficient resources, etc. These adversely affect quality of their deliverables. Microlearning perfectly counters these challenges as it does not demand big time commitments, huge infrastructure, enormous budgets and more importantly, it's 'learning'- comes 'from within' and not 'training'- bombarded 'from outside'! Microlearning is more than simply bite-sized learning assets. It allows employees to select and use learning assets most applicable to their current needs on whatever device is most handy, making the learning more relevant to their work. This learner-driven nature of Microlearning increases Engagement, Job Efficiency and Overall Learning ROI.

Abhijeet Mandlecha, Founder-CEO, Microstics

DOJOs

The term DOJO refers to fixed sessions lasting anywhere from an hour to an hour and a half, including a minimum forty-five minutes of coding Whatever time leftover is to be used for a brief retrospective. In this retrospective, a facilitator leads the participants, encouraging them to do the kata work in teams of two.

Programmers come to a coding DOJO to improve their skills While in a DOJO, people come with an openness to learn, accept constructive criticism, defend their ideas and explain their rationale and also teach others what they have learned and how they have evolved. Small code katas are solved at DOJOs.

Why Assess?

The main objective of having a DOJO is that people come together and unlearn to learn new aspects of coding and design to take away good practices and innovative thinking. The objective of assessment is to understand if the DOJOs are truly serving their purpose in reality

Key Practice Summary

3
Practice
DOJOs
DevOps Discipline Mapping
* Enterprise Design for DevOps *Continuous Learning
Focus Groups
*Application Teams *Technical Architects *Agile and DevOps Coaches
Example Inputs
*Learning Mechanisms *Application of Learning Outcomes *Best practices evangelization *Focussed problem solving *Exploring Patterns and Discovering Anti-patterns

Assessment Questions

**Questions to be scored on a scale of 1 to 5 (5 being ideal)*

***OSNA implies Objective Score Not Applicable*

	Question	Score
1.	To what extent are coding DOJOs designed as per principles?	1 2 3 4 5
2.	To what extent are DOJOs hosted in a stress-free ecosystem, with no agenda and no mandated deliverables?	1 2 3 4 5
3.	To what extent do DOJOs foster active and engaging participation with more volunteers to teach and learn?	1 2 3 4 5
4.	To what extent are the outcomes of every DOJO successfully leveraged for continual improvement?	1 2 3 4 5
5.	To what extent are collaboration games or frameworks leveraged during DOJOs?	1 2 3 4 5
6.	To what extent are technical practices like Test Driven Development (TDD), Behaviour Driven Development (BDD), etc. discussed and implemented in Coding DOJOs?	1 2 3 4 5
7.	To what extent do DOJOs have constructive retrospectives and healthy discussions focused on improvement?	1 2 3 4 5

Leaders Think

DOJO, a Japanese term traditionally used in the field of martial arts, has been increasingly applied now-a-days in agile software development – Coding DOJOs, Coaching DOJOs. At its core, a DOJO is a cultural movement involving learning, the spreading of knowledge and the application of that knowledge to improve organizations. In the technology world, DevOps DOJOs focus on a team goal or capability, cultivating cultural change and the new practices and technologies needed to achieve that goal or capability. Engineers are joined by coaches or masters in a dedicated workspace, like a traditional DOJO hall, to iteratively work through improve product planning, development, automation and delivery. Teams are empowered to take responsibility for quality while driving towards better, faster and higher quality products.

Atulya Pradhan, Transformation Champion, Capgemini

Adaptive Release Planning and Orchestration

For an organization to be a true DevOps organization, it has to be lean and agile. It has to have the ability to release on demand. Assessment of this area allows teams to understand their strength and weaknesses and identifies the dimension which requires attention and improvement.

Why Assess?

Release Planning and Orchestration are important from a DevOps Assesment perspective for a number of reasons.

- It enables an understanding of how the business requirements are prioritized and what are the kind of trade-offs established between business needs and development teams delivering the solution/product.
- It enables an understanding of complex business requirements that are worked on and split in collaboration with the customer.
- It facilitates an understanding of how releases are planned and orchestrated with distributed teams spread across multiple geographies, complex architectural landscape and multiple technical and functional dependencies across the entire solution landscape.
- It enables a fair degree of adaptiveness in the overall release planning.

Key Practice Summary

4

Practice

Adaptive Release Planning and Orchestration

DevOps Discipline Mapping

*DevOps Culture
*Enterprise Design for DevOps

Focus Groups

*Application Teams
*Technical Architects

Example Inputs

*Release Plan in Jenkins, JIRA and other tools used

Assessment Questions

**Questions to be scored on a scale of 1 to 5 (5 being ideal)*

***OSNA implies Objective Score Not Applicable*

Question	Score
1. What is the frequency of release cycle?	**OSNA
2. To what extent is a standard process for release management (covering change request and approval) defined and adhered to?	1 2 3 4 5
3. To what extent are the technical team members together with the Product Owner deciding which features should define the release scope?	1 2 3 4 5
4. Is there a mechanism established and implemented for tracking from requirements to release built within the delivery pipeline?	**OSNA
5. To what extent are technical dependencies and impediments discussed as part of the scope definition exercise for Release planning?	1 2 3 4 5
6. To what extent as a step towards continuous delivery, have you adopted any mechanisms such as "feature toggling" for derisking features that aren't business ready for production environments?	1 2 3 4 5

7. To what extent is "progressive exposure" adapted for new features developed and deployed?	① ② ③ ④ ⑤
8. For multiple releases that are happening in parallel for a large program, what are the practices followed to get fast feedback and refine the product/solution?	**OSNA
9. In the case of ring-based deployments being practiced, how do you arrive at the blast radius being set?	**OSNA
10. To what extent do your teams practice feature based releases and deployments?	① ② ③ ④ ⑤
11. To what extent is testing fully automated (unit, functional, load, regression and performance) at every stage across the SDLC?	① ② ③ ④ ⑤
12. To what extent do you have a built-in tracing within the delivery pipeline with auto-generated release notes?	① ② ③ ④ ⑤
13. To what extent can your teams consistently handle complex, multi-tier application delivery for many app teams' work across complex infrastructure and complex services without having to rely on the development of customized scripts or manual processing?	① ② ③ ④ ⑤
14. To what extent are your app delivery pipelines fully automated end-to-end across development, test and production environments?	① ② ③ ④ ⑤
15. To what extent are your delivery, promotion and release processes fully automated?	① ② ③ ④ ⑤
16. To what extent are your app delivery pipeline processes fully automated, interconnected and integrated?	① ② ③ ④ ⑤
17. To what extent are self-service roll-in and rollback built within the delivery pipeline?	① ② ③ ④ ⑤
18. To what extent can your monitoring practices scale to manage modern app architectures built upon a mix of containerized apps, cloud-based microservices and software-defined networks?	① ② ③ ④ ⑤
19. To what extent do your releases catering to multiple user groups adapt practices like canary release?	① ② ③ ④ ⑤
20. To what extent is dependency management done using a repository?	① ② ③ ④ ⑤

Leaders Think

Adaptive release planning is about delivering value predictably. Taking an adaptive approach to your Release Planning process will help you achieve the goals in your release plan, allowing you to be more confident in your commitments. As technology evolves and people continue to learn from our people-centric DevOps process, our release management processes need to change too. The continuous improvement of people, processes and technology is essential to any successful adaptive release management. After capturing your baseline assessment begin to create your improvement plan by using hypothesis driven experiments to improve areas in your assessment that were identified as less than ideal.Anyone trying to move changes out to production can benefit from release orchestration. Orchestration products implement delivery pipelines based on templates, using these templates you can always feel confident that a consistent, repeatable process is being followed every time you run your release. Feedback from retrospectives of previous releases can be easily integrated into future releases, ensuring that each release runs a bit better and is a bit more reliable than the previous ones.

Tracy Bridenbaugh, CEO/Digital Transformation Leader,
Tracy Bridenbaugh and Associates

Metrics

DevOps is all about continuous delivery and shipping of the code in a continuous manner. To move as fast as possible, it is important to be able to assess the progress of how DevOps and that's the objective of metrics.

Why Assess?

- Enables stakeholders to assess the progress of DevOps in the organization and leverage the feedback for course corrections
- Enables data-driven continuous improvement across the organization

Key Practice Summary

5
Practice
Metrics
DevOps Discipline Mapping
*Enterprise Design for DevOps *Continuous Learning
Focus Groups
* Application Teams *Scrum Masters *Agile and DevOps Coaches
Example Inputs
*Metrics Dashboards in Excel, Tableau and other Visualization Tools *Pipeline Analytics in Jenkins, JIRA and other tools *Manually reported Metrics *Automated Reports generated by tools like SonarQube

Assessment Questions

**Questions to be scored on a scale of 1 to 5 (5 being ideal)*

***OSNA implies Objective Score Not Applicable*

	Question	Score
1.	To what extent do your metrics facilitate real-time discovery of problems and incident analytics?	1 2 3 4 5
2.	To what extent do your metrics indicate a true picture of progress and predictability of the release status of your application?	1 2 3 4 5
3.	What is the degree of automation implemented (Automated Tests Pass%)?	1 2 3 4 5
4.	How often do changes in code cause the automated tests to break(Rate 5 for no breaks caused)?	1 2 3 4 5
5.	What is the extent of SLA(Service Level Agreements) compliance for the said application?	1 2 3 4 5
6.	To what extent do your IT services or products fail during critical times?	1 2 3 4 5
7.	To what extent are your critical business processes covered by a service availability plan?	1 2 3 4 5
8.	To what extent do your metrics dashboards visualize topology, deployment activities and the operational state showing availability and performance metrics for various applications?	1 2 3 4 5
9.	To what extent do your metrics dashboards visualize the key service indicators from a user perspective?	1 2 3 4 5
10.	What is your deployment size and frequency? And what are the targets you aim to achieve leveraging DevOps as an enabler?	**OSNA
11.	What is the time it takes to complete a deployment?	**OSNA
12.	What is an average lead time that it takes to get a feature from being listed on the backlog to production?	**OSNA
13.	What is the volume of support tickets raised on the application by the customer or end user after the code is deployed to production?	**OSNA
14.	What is the Defect Escape Rate to production?	**OSNA
15.	What is the Application/Service availability?	**OSNA
16.	Any potential areas of concerns? Any SLA breaches that need attention?	**OSNA

17. What is the Mean Time between Failures (MTBF)?	**OSNA
18. In the case of microservices architecture, how are you tracking application usage and traffic?	**OSNA

Leaders Think

Generate some initial insights and display these on dashboards which are essential for tracking metrics all in one place. Start by capturing metrics that are simpler to collect and manage. For better focus, don't apply too many metrics. Choose metrics that fit your business model. Strive to capture your measurements as fast as possible to enable near real-time feedback loops. The insights that you gain from these metrics should allow you to work with your team to inspect and adapt incrementally. Prioritize the metric to improve based on the one which will provide the highest overall improvement from the actions taken based on the improved metric.

Tracy Bridenbaugh, CEO / Digital Transformation Leader,
Tracy Bridenbaugh and Associates

Managing DevOps metrics is vital as these give insights into what is happening at all stages of DevOps pipeline from design to development to deployment. Since DevOps is cross-functional (process,people,tools) and across teams(dev,ops,testing) metrics for DevOps should not narrow their focus on only some parts of the value chain. Metrics should capture a holistic view of entire value chain. The major metrics of focus is Metrics for application build cycles ,metrics for application performance, metrics for delivery performance, metrics organized by infrastructure ,system and team health and metrics for building or running apps.

Hariharasudan Sethumadavan, Senior Manager, Capgemini

Organization Design for Collaboration at Scale

A DevOps organization is a portmanteau of development and operations with collaboration across teams from idea to deployment.

Why Assess?

To understand how you should structure your organization to speed up value delivery while increasing organizational agility, it is important to redesign or restructure the organization to align it best with the needs of an Agile and DevOps organization. As organizations scale up, the number of teams working in silos increases multifold thereby creating communication blocks. It is here that organization design becomes an important area for DevOps.

Key Practice Summary

6

Practice

Organization Design for Collaboration at Scale

DevOps Discipline Mapping

*Enterprise Design for DevOps
*DevOps Culture

Focus Groups

*Application Teams
*Scrum Masters
*Agile and DevOps Coaches
*Technical Architects

Example Inputs

*DevOps - Roles and Responsibilities identifcation and adherence
*Team KPIs
*Talent Acquisition
*Program Review Mechanisms and Outcomes
*Leadership participation and support in DevOps pilots and progress
*Innovation think tanks

Assessment Questions

**Questions to be scored on a scale of 1 to 5 (5 being ideal)*

***OSNA implies Objective Score Not Applicable*

Question		Score
1.	To what extent do your performance appraisals, reward and recognition mechanisms establish a team culture successfully? Rate on a scale of 1 to 5 (1 for Superstar culture and 5 for team culture)	(1) (2) (3) (4) (5)
2.	To what extent do your hiring mechanisms align with building a DevOps organization?	(1) (2) (3) (4) (5)
3.	To what extent is your recruitment process agile?	(1) (2) (3) (4) (5)
4.	To what extent are your hiring specialists incentivized to liaise with business and close the hiring within a stipulated titme? Look out for the onboarding times of new hires.	(1) (2) (3) (4) (5)
5.	To what extent do your organizational systems reward the DevOps behaviours?	(1) (2) (3) (4) (5)
6.	What is HR's role and extent of involvement in overall in the organization's transformation journey?	(1) (2) (3) (4) (5)
7.	The organization is embracing DevOps, but its HR processes are still functioning in the traditional way and unable to support or further build its agility. Can that and should that change? How?	**OSNA
8.	How does the function of HR change on this journey?	**OSNA
9.	What does it mean for you and your team in HR to adopt a DevOps mindset?	**OSNA
10.	What changes do are being brought to your traditional HR processes and how?	**OSNA
11.	How do your recruitment, learning and development, performance management and employee motivation and engagement change with this change being driven in the organization?	**OSNA
12.	Do you need to upgrade your own skills to drive or be a part of this DevOps transformation?	**OSNA
13.	.Do you continue to do annual appraisals or do you approach goal setting and performance management differently going forward?	**OSNA

Leaders Think

It is a common misconception that DevOps is all about tools, code and infrastructure. For any DevOp implementation to be successful, it is important to redesign and retrofit our organization. Traditional silo-based organization structure will not work, if the organization wants to achieve effectiveness and efficiency through DevOps. The organization design has to be a perfect balance between lean, lightweight and at the same time flexible enough to scale upwards as the transformation dimension increases. Organization design has to incorporate aspects of Psychological safety, Risk taking ability, Adaptability & overall alignment to Agile culture and mindset.

Ashutosh Bhatawadekar, Enterprise Agile Consultant,
Tata Consultancy Services

What an interesting topic to think about and pretty much prevalent in today's time of globalized workplaces! We are leaving in a world where every day, everyone has to be an efficient communicator, active listener and eloquent writer to communicate at scale with colleagues sitting across different continents. What I am saying indirectly is, we need efficient collaboration at scale to improve on generating results that matter and organizational design plays major role in realizing this goal. DevOps forces organization to engage in close collaboration if embraced to its true spirit! Despite of an availability of tools and technologies which have substantially reduced the physical separation among work colleagues, it is not sufficient for achieving true collaboration at scale. Organizational design must reflect flatter hierarchy, reduced handoff of a work between teams and departments, faster decision making with requisite inclusion of important stakeholders and most importantly close customer collaboration! And you please tell me, if a leadership team which has sincerely created and clearly communicated company's vision and backed it up by offering psychological safety to teams for their failures in realizing the dream, wouldn't that lead to an achievement of collaboration at scale?

Akhil Bhansali, Founder and CEO, AgileBeings

DevOps Contracting Models

Customers often outsource complex application and systems development to partner or supplier organizations who can build these. There's a spectrum of approaches and options to contracting, ranging from fixed price to time and materials, with a host of conditions in between. Understanding this becomes crucial to translating them in objectives and priorities for the teams that also to an extent defines the team's ways of working.

Why Assess?

Assessing DevOps Contracts is essential for multiple reasons.

- It optimizes the business value for all stakeholders in both the short and long-term
- It exploits facilitates adaptive responses to changing customer requirements as new knowledge emerges
- It provides complete transparency, visibility and objectivity of solution fitness
- It provides a measured and low-risk approach to investment that can vary with time and stop when sufficient value has been achieved
- It offers the supplier the immediate confidence of short-term funding and sufficient notice when funding winds diminish
- It motivates all parties to an optimal solution feasible within agreed-to economic boundaries

Key Practice Summary

7	
Practice	
DevOps Contracting Models	
DevOps Discipline Mapping	
*DevOps Mindset *DevOps Culture *Enterprise Design for DevOps	
Focus Groups	
*Application Teams *Scrum Masters *Agile and DevOps Coaches *Technical Architects *Portfolio Managers *Program Managers *Vice Presidents	*CIOS *Business Leaders *Procurement team (where applicable) *Legal team (where applicable) *Sales and Marketing (where applicable)
Example Inputs	
*Contracts, MSAs, SOWs *Funding Model *Service Delivery Model *RACI	

Assessment Questions

**Questions to be scored on a scale of 1 to 5 (5 being ideal)*

***OSNA implies Objective Score Not Applicable*

Question		Score
1.	To what extent do the present contracts for projects or programs executed the DevOps way exhibit commitment based models as basis of contracting?	1 2 3 4 5
2.	To what extent are traditional project life cycle activities like requirements gathering and management, estimation, change management, signoffs, etc. aligned with the DevOps and Agile approach?	1 2 3 4 5
3.	To what extent are the acceptance criteria jointly identified by the customer and the development team together? And is this collaboration agreed contractually for the entire duration of the project or product?	1 2 3 4 5
4.	To what extent does the contract reflect an agreement by both– the customer and the supplier that no changes except those that are business critical and regulatory in nature will be incorporated within an iteration post iteration planning?	1 2 3 4 5
5.	To what extent does the contract lay a cap on the sizing of any exceptional changes introduced within an iteration post iteration planning? For example, such changes can be 1 or 2 story points per iteration maximum.	1 2 3 4 5

6.	To what extent is it contractually agreed that the supplier team will not pick up work from the product backlog (epic, feature or story) if it does not meet the Definition of Ready?	(1) (2) (3) (4) (5)
7.	To what extent is it contractually agreed on marking a feature completion post completion of all stories within the feature that comply with the definition of done?	(1) (2) (3) (4) (5)
8.	To what extent does the contract indicate an adherence to agile cadences for iterations and releases with an active collaboration between the Customer and supplier or the product development team?	(1) (2) (3) (4) (5)
9.	To what extent does the contract ensure that any third-party dependencies (e.g., hardware/software procurement, regulatory/compliance clearances, etc.) are aligned with the agreed timelines of releases?	(1) (2) (3) (4) (5)

Leaders Think

Today's VUCA digital world demands organizations to embrace a change mindset to be able to adapt to the DevOps ways of working in order to successfully transform their business landscape with this philosophy. But that's not all. Just the core functions of development and operations embracing DevOps will not create a true DevOps organization. In other words, other business enabling functions like procurement, legal, human resources, marketing and sales also need to understand and speak the DevOps lingo.

When it comes to engaging in project or program contracts that demand such transformation, it may be a good idea to move away from a traditional milestone-based approach to a value-and-risk sharing driven approach. In other words, the responsibility for DevOps success becomes a shared goal of both the customer and the supplier. This translates into shift in focus from outputs to outcomes. KPIs are attached to business outcomes. There may be a risk and reward agreement between both parties on how to move forward with the existential uncertainties. Sometimes organizations also choose to use hybrid models that use time and material for some part of the overall program scope lending consulting expertise and time and risk sharing for a limited piece of the scope. Overall, outcome-based contracting for DevOps drives effective governance, solution quality and speeds up the delivery while also mitigating the risk.

- Sonal Drone, Managing Consultant, IBM

Technical Practices, Tools and Processes

Technical Practices, Tools and Processes

Why Do Technical Practices, Tools and Processes matter to DevOps?

Technical practices are key to an effective DevOps implementation but with the right culture. Most organizations are fighting a cultural battle and not a technological one.

Assessment Objectives

- They enable development of a cleaner, extensible and maintainable code with higher product quality
- They enable achieving higher product quality and faster time to market

Key Practices Summary

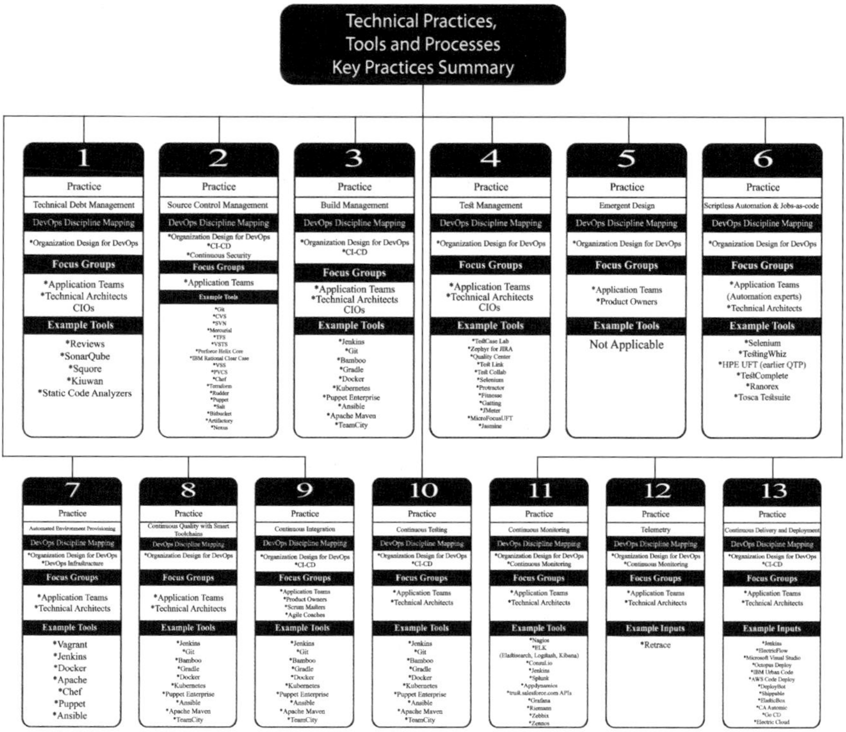

Technical Debt Management

Technical debt, in a nutshell, is bad code, bad design practices and increasingly complex code, all of which account for significant rework and refactoring to automate and find better solutions to make the software more maintainable. Thus said, technical debt management becomes a key practice for effective DevOps.

Why Assess?

- Enables a more maintainable software
- Enables mitigating the business risk by having focused effort and resources invested where needed to make an impact
- Reduces code complexity and thus significant potential rework effort in future

Key Practice Summary

1
Practice
Technical Debt Management
DevOps Discipline Mapping
*Organization Design for DevOps
Focus Groups
*Application Teams *Technical Architects CIOs
Example Tools
*Reviews *SonarQube *Squore *Kiuwan *Static Code Analyzers

Assessment Questions

**Questions to be scored on a scale of 1 to 5 (5 being ideal)*

***OSNA implies Objective Score Not Applicable*

Question	Score
1. How is technical debt managed within the Program?	**OSNA
2. To what extent is reduction of technical debt integrated with the overall CI strategy?	① ② ③ ④ ⑤
3. To what extent does the team dedicate a fixed percentage of time every iteration to improve the technical debt on a continual basis?	① ② ③ ④ ⑤
4. What is the extent to which refactoring is deployed as an engineering practice for technical excellence?	① ② ③ ④ ⑤
5. Are code smells detected as part of the Technical Audits or Code Reviews that have been conducted so far? If yes, how have these been addressed?	**OSNA
6. Are pair programming methods used for coding?	**OSNA
7. To what extent are newer services written using practices like Test Driven Development (TDD)?	① ② ③ ④ ⑤
8. To what extent are techniques like Behaviour Driven Development (BDD) used to create the scenarios that demonstrate system behaviour?	① ② ③ ④ ⑤
9. To what extent is your code written in a modular fashion?	① ② ③ ④ ⑤
10. What is the extent of current code complexity? (1 being must complex and 5 being ideal)	① ② ③ ④ ⑤
11. To what extent are there measures and practices in place to simplify code complexity? Look out for examples.	① ② ③ ④ ⑤
12. To what extent are there established mechanisms for ensuring test coverage and functional code coverage?	① ② ③ ④ ⑤
13. What are the code quality metrics, usability metrics and data quality metrics that illustrate the extent of existing technical debt?	**OSNA
14. To what extent are your integration patterns and technologies leveraged for pipeline orchestration standardized? Rate on a scale of 1 to 5 (5 being most standardized)	① ② ③ ④ ⑤
15. To what extent is your team customizing any of the standardized integration patterns that are creating "tool debt" for addressing later? (5 being most customization being done)	① ② ③ ④ ⑤
16. To what extent is model-based integration used to prevent disruption of workflows when old tools are replaced with new tools? Rate on a scale of 1 to 5 (5 being model-based integration is commonly practiced)	① ② ③ ④ ⑤

Leaders Think

Technical debt in organizations can be compared to monetary debt and is made for the sake of expediency. Its definitely not good inherently but it can lead to conversations around better ways to deliver software, increase automation, implement better and leaner processes, make code more maintainable and so on.

Technical debt definitely reflects the implied cost of additional rework that might be caused by choosing an easy workaround around limited solutions now instead of taking a better solution that would require a longer path to implement. It also might be because of time constraints placed on the development itself, source code complexity, poor design decisions or business decisions that lack clarity on the part of the business.

Technical debt if not managed continuously can increase in a compounded fashion. Hence, it is important to work on it in a continuous and agile manner with an objective to reduce it. Technical debt governance should be part of the culture. Be proactive about it, have metrics that capture it, have open conversations about technical debt with leadership and I think you will be able to address it very effectively.

Padmini Nidumolu, Co-Founder , Lean-in-Agile

Source Control Management

Source control management, also known as version control management, is a key practice that enables tracking and managing changes to code, scripts and other configurable artifacts throughout the software development lifecycle. It provides an audit trail by providing a running history of code development and facilitates resolution of conflicts when merging files from multiple branches.

Why Assess?

- Source Code Management (SCM) and version control systems ensure all members of a team stay on top of changes to source code and related files.
- Enables an integral management of files across multiple teams with the versions controlled and an audit trail for any modifications made to any of the files
- Enables rollback to previous working versions in case of change failure
- Helps in coordinating parallel work on multiple features and the integration of the features for different software releases

Key Practice Summary

2
Practice
Source Control Management
DevOps Discipline Mapping
*Organization Design for DevOps *CI-CD *Continuous Security
Focus Groups
*Application Teams
Example Tools
*Git *CVS *SVN *Mercurial *TFS *VSTS *Perforce Helix Core *IBM Rational Clear Case *VSS *PVCS *Chef *Terraform *Rudder *Puppet *Salt *Bitbucket *Artifactory *Nexus

Assessment Questions

**Questions to be scored on a scale of 1 to 5 (5 being ideal)*

***OSNA implies Objective Score Not Applicable*

Question	Score
1. To what extent do you ensure changes in the source code are in version control and communicated and annotated transparently for the whole team?	① ② ③ ④ ⑤
2. How do you manage branching and labeling? Do you have a well-defined and documented branching, tagging and merging strategy?	**OSNA
3. How do you ensure that the current production release can be patched while continuing to develop new features?	**OSNA
4. To what extent do you ensure authenticated access for commits?	① ② ③ ④ ⑤
5. To what extent do you ensure revision history on files is updated?	① ② ③ ④ ⑤
6. To what extent do you ensure atomic commits of multiple files?	① ② ③ ④ ⑤
7. To what extent do you ensure source code, application configurations, environment configurations and build scripts are all under source control?	① ② ③ ④ ⑤
8. How frequent (number of times per developer) are your code commits in a day?	**OSNA
9. How do you ensure that the code that is locally built is the latest, unit-tested and code-reviewed before commit (pre-tested commit)? What are the code quality checks in place?	**OSNA
10. How frequently (number of times a day) is your mainline updated?	**OSNA
11. To what extent do you ensure database scripts including schema and data are all under source control?	① ② ③ ④ ⑤
12. To what extent do you ensure that your commits (changes) are tied to tasks or defects?	① ② ③ ④ ⑤
13. To what extent are tests linked to a defined requirement or story?	① ② ③ ④ ⑤
14. To what extent do you store all the binary artifacts in a versioned source repository?	① ② ③ ④ ⑤
15. To what extent are application and environment configurations externalized from code and are each maintained separate?	① ② ③ ④ ⑤
16. To what extent do you use a version control mechanism for all elements of your delivery pipeline?	① ② ③ ④ ⑤
17. To what extent are your database scripts (schema, data) in version control?	① ② ③ ④ ⑤

18.	To what extent do you have "Infrastructure as Code" stored in the source control system?	① ② ③ ④ ⑤

Leaders Think

The thought at the top of my mind when someone uses the term Source Control Management is typically a traditional system like VSS, SVN or a newer distributed system like Git. Although, in true sense source control has a humanistic angle as well. It's all about maintaining transparency and improving team collaboration while also maintaining an audit trail for easy rollbacks and recovery in case of change failures. It enables everyone in the team to keep in synch with the latest changes to the code and understand the impact of any change on all related files so as to effectively merge contributions from different branches or sources and resolve conflicts. It is a critical practice that is absolutely key to a successful DevOps culture.

Amit Naidu, Technical Program Lead, Wolterskluwer

Build Management

Build management is a key practice by which a software product for an organization is built and managed. Build Automation is the key to implementing successful DevOps.

Why Assess?

Build management is important to ensure early detection of errors while integrating changes. This, in turn, saves both time and money from the perspective of rework and failure. As the team matures, they move from manual towards automated builds thereby minimizing any errors due to human intervention.

Key Practice Summary

3

Practice

Build Management

DevOps Discipline Mapping

*Organization Design for DevOps
*CI-CD

Focus Groups

*Application Teams
*Technical Architects
CIOs

Example Tools

*Jenkins
*Git
*Bamboo
*Gradle
*Docker
*Kubernetes
*Puppet Enterprise
*Ansible
*Apache Maven
*TeamCity

Assessment Questions

**Questions to be scored on a scale of 1 to 5 (5 being ideal)*

***OSNA implies Objective Score Not Applicable*

Question		Score
1.	To what extent are official builds are performed on separate build machines?	(1) (2) (3) (4) (5)
2.	To what extent is there a standard build process (compile, UT, FT and KPIs) defined for local and central build?	(1) (2) (3) (4) (5)
3.	To what extent are there common build scripts for local as well as central build (and also include UT, FT and meet KPIs) and pre-tested build.	(1) (2) (3) (4) (5)
4.	To what extent is the code polled from source control and build on commit?	(1) (2) (3) (4) (5)
5.	To what extent are build artifacts managed through a repository with versioning?	(1) (2) (3) (4) (5)
6.	To what extent are build notifications configured (for success as well as for failure KPIs)?	(1) (2) (3) (4) (5)
7.	To what extent is there a build dashboard defined, providing built status and KPIs details?	(1) (2) (3) (4) (5)
8.	To what extent is the versioning and tagging of code automated and part of the build process?	(1) (2) (3) (4) (5)
9.	To what extent are triggered builds (no polling) for each code commit into version control?	(1) (2) (3) (4) (5)
10.	How do you manage distributed builds on build cluster?	**OSNA
11.	To what extent do you have a build environment on virtual machines?	(1) (2) (3) (4) (5)
12.	To what extent do you have gated commits?	(1) (2) (3) (4) (5)

Leaders Think

Build management, typically is a workflow comprised of a set of tools that build, compile, package and version code that enables teams to redistribute the code as needed. This includes a Build Console, Source Code Repository and Package Repository. Efficient build management practices detect errors early, enable open communication, enhance team collaboration and improve overall product release quality.

Amit Naidu, Technical Program Lead, Wolterskluwer

Test Management

Test management for DevOps is a practice of managing manual and automated test cases. It enables DevOps teams to work with enhanced collaboration making the entire test management workflow more lean and nimble through practices like automated build, automated testing and automated provisioning of infrastructure for deployment in order to reduce time to market for the entire release.

Why Assess?

Test Case Management is crucial in DevOps in terms of overall improving the scope and functional coverage of testing as well as improving the testing efficiency. An efficient test management mechanism also provides inputs to the test cases that are good candidates for automation thereby harnessing the benefits of DevOps.

Key Practice Summary

4
Practice
Test Management
DevOps Discipline Mapping
*Organization Design for DevOps
Focus Groups
*Application Teams *Technical Architects CIOs
Example Tools
*TestCase Lab *Zephyr for JIRA *Quality Center *Test Link *Test Collab *Selenium *Protractor *Fitnesse *Gatting *JMeter *MicroFocusUFT *Jasmine

Assessment Questions

**Questions to be scored on a scale of 1 to 5 (5 being ideal)*

***OSNA implies Objective Score Not Applicable*

Question	Score
1. To what extent is automated unit testing part of the local and central build?	① ② ③ ④ ⑤
2. To what extent is there a standard testing process (UT, FT, IT, PT, UAT and KPIs) defined and implemented across all teams?	① ② ③ ④ ⑤
3. To what extent are all test artifacts peer-reviewed?	① ② ③ ④ ⑤
4. To what extent are KPIs measured with significant coverage?	① ② ③ ④ ⑤
5. To what extent are notifications configured for each kind of testing?	① ② ③ ④ ⑤
6. To what extent are mocks used for external test dependencies?	① ② ③ ④ ⑤
7. To what extent is unit testing and smoke testing on each commit a part of the build process?	① ② ③ ④ ⑤
8. To what extent is the functional testing automated?	① ② ③ ④ ⑤
9. To what extent do you achieve dynamic functional test coverage?	① ② ③ ④ ⑤
10. To what extent is test data management and maintenance an integral part of your DevOps strategy?	① ② ③ ④ ⑤
11. To what extent are service virtualization capabilities built?	① ② ③ ④ ⑤
12. To what extent is the non-functional testing automated?	① ② ③ ④ ⑤
13. To what extent have you achieved UAT automation?	① ② ③ ④ ⑤

Leaders Think

Test Management tools should be robust and scalable to meet the growing needs of the enterprise. With increased automation, the databases of test code and test case load both grow exponentially. It is here that such tools should ensure maximum degree of availability and reliability and provide full deployments to meet enterprise testing needs, be it on-premise server, cloud, distributed network or data centers.

Umesh Jain, Vice President, Deutsche Bank Group

Emergent Design

Emergent design is a design that is constructed as it evolves as opposed to the usual upfront process of design. It enables design to evolve as the solution gets clearer with an evolving solution architecture.

Why Assess?

- Enables design to emerge accommodating changes in solution architecture
- Enables more robust and scalable product or solution design through focusing on end state future requirements than focusing on mere functionality and features

Key Practice Summary

5
Practice
Emergent Design
DevOps Discipline Mapping
*Organization Design for DevOps
Focus Groups
*Application Teams *Product Owners
Example Tools
Not Applicable

Assessment Questions

**Questions to be scored on a scale of 1 to 5 (5 being ideal)*

***OSNA implies Objective Score Not Applicable*

Question		Score
1.	To what extent does your team do sufficient just-in-time planning on design to progress with the iteration tasks?	① ② ③ ④ ⑤
2.	To what extent does your team leverage the principles of continuous architecture to establish emergent design? Look out for examples.	① ② ③ ④ ⑤
3.	To what extent does your design reflect being developed with a JEDI (Just Enough Design Initially) mindset further relying upon the core experience and skills of team members and broadly accepted patterns?	① ② ③ ④ ⑤
4.	To what extent are untested assumptions and inconsistent technical architectures constantly validated or discussed and addressed by the teams?	① ② ③ ④ ⑤
5.	Is the design orchestrated in silos or has it evolved with some intentional architecture from the perspective of enhancing solution design, performance and usability to provide crossteam design and implementation synchronization? (This may particularly be applicable and important to large-scale programs/projects getting influenced in mergers and acquisitions)	**OSNA
6.	To what extent is design debt addressed?	① ② ③ ④ ⑤
7.	What are the mechanisms used to identify design debt (e.g., change vector tracking)?	**OSNA
8.	How do you track design debt particularly for microservices added on existing architecture (Lookout for change vector tracking mechanisms or similar)?	**OSNA
9.	In present context, what are the "wicked" problems that your emergent design is trying to address?	**OSNA

Leaders Think

The DevOps philosophy builds on business agility with focus on iterative and incremental value delivery. It strikes an optimal balance between intentional architecture and emergent design. Emergent design enables robust and scalable architectural governance while creating a technical basis for a pragmatic implementation approach that is evolutionary as well as emergent and responsive to the needs of the business. Emergent design of a system or product together with proper architectural governance can enable designing products that is futuristic with a focus on end to end requirements than a myopic focus on specific functionalities.

Sonal Drone, Managing Consultant, IBM

Scriptless Automation and Jobs-as-Code

Test automation has always been attractive because it reduces the manual and rulebased testing efforts and accelerates testing. Nearly every organization automates its test cases, but the ROI does not always turn out as had been expected.

Scriptless test automation is like shopping for fruit: only the best apples get picked. The rotten ones get let behind. This frees business users and testers to automate test cases without needing to focus so much on the coding aspects, as the scriptless automation tool will mostly do the grunt work of this. It helps achieve quicker results and reduces the time spent to dig deep and understand the code.

Why Assess?

- Allows improved stakeholder collaboration (business analysts, SMEs, customers) during test automation making automation simpler and easier
- Reduces time to automate significantly
- Enables higher test coverage
- Eliminates coding that is tool-specific

Key Practice Summary

6
Practice
Scriptless Automation & Jobs-as-code
DevOps Discipline Mapping
*Organization Design for DevOps
Focus Groups
*Application Teams (Automation experts) *Technical Architects
Example Tools
*Selenium *TestingWhiz *HPE UFT (earlier QTP) *TestComplete *Ranorex *Tosca Testsuite

Assessment Questions

**Questions to be scored on a scale of 1 to 5 (5 being ideal)*

***OSNA implies Objective Score Not Applicable*

Question		Score
1.	What role does the business play in setting development strategies within IT?	**OSNA
2.	How is automation integrated as a Shift Left mechanism in the overall strategy?	**OSNA
3.	To what extent is automation applied as a DevOps practice in teams?	① ② ③ ④ ⑤
4.	To what extent is automation effectively applied to create "Jobs-as-code"?	① ② ③ ④ ⑤
5.	To what extent is scriptless automation as a practice being practiced by your teams?	① ② ③ ④ ⑤
6.	Is culture change a requirement or a result of doing DevOps?	**OSNA
7.	What are the benefits of doing DevOps automation?	**OSNA
8.	To what extent does your present level of automation allow you to get quick, real-time and automated feedback on the production readiness of your systems?	① ② ③ ④ ⑤
9.	To what extent can you perform push button or zero touch deployments with any version of the software to any environment on demand?	① ② ③ ④ ⑤
10.	To what extent does your team constantly prioritize while keeping the release deployable over working on new features?	① ② ③ ④ ⑤
11.	To what extent does DevOps bring value to your business?	① ② ③ ④ ⑤
12.	To what extent is IT flexible enough to support DevOps?	① ② ③ ④ ⑤
13.	To what extent can the organization commit to constant change?	① ② ③ ④ ⑤

Leaders Think

Scriptless Automation is creation of codeless automated test scenarios leveraging the business knowledge of manual testers. It is quick to implement, enables faster test creation and execution while also reducing maintenance costs significantly providing an immediate time to value. Most frameworks integrate and leverage modules developed by the community. It allows early defect detection, frequent releases and integrates with the delivery pipeline improving the overall quality of digital products.

Amit Naidu, Technical Program Lead, Wolterskluwer

Automated Environment Provisioning

Environment provisioning is how an organization manages infrastructure before, during and after the lifespan of an application or service. It is a key part of a continuous delivery process. Environments consist of infrastructure, configuration and dependencies. With organizations embracing virtualization and infrastructure on demand, configuration and provisioning of environments has moved from days to seconds.

Why Assess?

- Improved provisioning cycle time
- Significant reduction in manual health check efforts
- Improved efficiency of the environment via reducing fulfillment requests for IT service
- Reduced cost of operations
- Eliminates configuration drift
- Eliminates errors due to manual interventions and lags due to dependencies
- Facilitates zero tolerance for non-availability of the environment
- Integral environments through automated configuration updates that are consistent and accurate
- Promotes utilization of infrastructure assets optimally through improved license management
- Enables environment as a service model applicable where needed
- Minimizes revenue leakage

Key Practice Summary

7
Practice
Automated Environment Provisioning
DevOps Discipline Mapping
*Organization Design for DevOps *DevOps Infrastructure
Focus Groups
*Application Teams *Technical Architects
Example Tools
*Vagrant *Jenkins *Docker *Apache *Chef *Puppet *Ansible

Assessment Questions

**Questions to be scored on a scale of 1 to 5 (5 being ideal)*

***OSNA implies Objective Score Not Applicable*

Question	Score
1. How is environment agility considered while designing environments?	**OSNA
2. How is environment efficiency tracked and measured?	**OSNA
3. How is environment stability tracked and measured?	**OSNA
4. To what extent are you able to continuously adapt to transition to workloads – up and down?	① ② ③ ④ ⑤
5. To what extent is your release and deployment process across all environments standardized?	① ② ③ ④ ⑤

6.	To what extent are the infrastructure provisioning scripts under source control?	① ② ③ ④ ⑤
7.	To what extent do you have a standardized process for branching, tagging, versioning and merging, etc., defined and implemented across all applications and environments?	① ② ③ ④ ⑤
8.	To what extent are application and environment configurations externalized from code?	① ② ③ ④ ⑤
9.	To what extent are applications and environments capable of autoscaling when needed?	① ② ③ ④ ⑤
10.	To what extent do you have push button deployments in place?	① ② ③ ④ ⑤
11.	To what extent do you have blue-green deployments in place for monolithic applications planned for re-architecting, replatforming and reengineering?	① ② ③ ④ ⑤
12.	To what extent do you have metrics defined, gathered and reported for utilization and billing of environment and infrastructure usage?	① ② ③ ④ ⑤
13.	To what extent do you have patching and upgrades automated?	① ② ③ ④ ⑤
14.	To what extent do you have mechanisms for performance monitoring and assisted self-healing in place?	① ② ③ ④ ⑤

Leaders Think

Automated provisioning, also called self-service provisioning, is the ability to deploy an information technology or telecommunications service by using pre-defined procedures that are carried out electronically without requiring human intervention.

The term provisioning, which originated in telecommunications, is the act of acquiring a service. In a traditional setting, provisioning is a manual process that requires the assistance of several people in several roles and involves multiple steps. It could take days or even weeks to move a request from the submission phase through the actual activation of service. Automating provisioning allows customers to set up and make changes to services themselves by using a web browser or other client interface. It can provide a more efficient and rapid response to business requests and cut service activation or service change time down to hours or even minutes.

Automated provisioning is a type of policy-based management and provisioning rights can be granted on either a permissions-based or role-based basis. Once automated provisioning has been implemented, it is up to the service provider to ensure that operational processes are being followed and governance policies are not being circumvented. Some of its key benefits include scalability, reduced error and revenue leakage and a single connected platform for all provisioning needs.

Raghunath Jawdekar, Independent Consultant

Automated environment provisioning arises from the need that code moves through multiple environments prior to moving to production. Each of these environments should be replica of each other so as to avoid gaps in the testing executed. For automated environment provisioning, there is an ideal state to be reached, that of a one-click install which brings the "unit-tested" and "integrated" underlying components together and once installed there is at least a functional sanity to be run to validate the install and certify the environment. With that ideal stage to reach, come all the assumptions which we start looking as "MUST HAVEs" to attempt automated environment provisioning. This makes the developers perceive this as an extremely complex activity which hence keeps getting de-prioritized. With an incremental approach, by breaking things down, things start looking simpler and achievable. A few tactics that have worked in some organizations I worked for:

1. Start with one integration environment that the team can refresh automatically every week as the first target
2. As a pre-requisite, familiarize your team with initialization and consolidation of install parameters and the basic high level design disciplines such as having good separation between code, data and configurations that will make your installers ready for increments along with your functional increments
3. Work with your team to identify platform and component versions that they will be working with
4. Ensure that the platform and these technical components can be built at an agreeable frequency

5. After discussing high level functionalities to be delivered in a release, with visibility till now, write down the code deliverables that the installers would consume (for example a jar, a package, a docker an rpm, Initialization or configuration scripts)
6. Coach your team to write the installers before the actual deliverables are ready as long as they spell out those deliverables in step #2. Once these installers are ready start introducing complexities of handling intra and intercomponent dependencies incrementally or using the same scripts to refresh multiple environments or to run a functional sanity to validate the environment.

So start small and let the team experience the value for themselves!

Prachi Saraph, Director-Engineering, Guavus Network Systems

Continuous Quality with Smart Toolchains

The very word "**DevOps**" recalls working functionalities delivered frequently to the customer through highly automated processes and a bunch of tools at different stages, all seamlessly integrated to facilitate idea to deployment in a very efficient and collaborative manner. Thus said, it is the toolchains in an enterprise that are the heart of DevOps, driving core technical practices like CI-CD and beyond.

Why Assess?

The very term "**DevOps**" brings to mind tools as critical building blocks that facilitate or enable the DevOps mindset from an implementation perspective. In real organizations, there are many tools that are standalone or not so well integrated with the rest of the ecosystem. These pose definite roadblocks or areas for opportunity.

While disparate tools do the job, they certainly slow down the overall DevOps velocity. Hence it becomes important to look at toolchains in the context of the overall DevOps organization.

Intelligent integration of toolchain can increase the value stream velocity of an organization and enable delivery of the best quality apps consistently

Key Practice Summary

8
Practice
Continuous Quality with Smart Toolchains
DevOps Discipline Mapping
*Organization Design for DevOps
Focus Groups
*Application Teams *Technical Architects
Example Tools
*Jenkins *Git *Bamboo *Gradle *Docker *Kubernetes *Puppet Enterprise *Ansible *Apache Maven *TeamCity

Assessment Questions

**Questions to be scored on a scale of 1 to 5 (5 being ideal)*

***OSNA implies Objective Score Not Applicable*

Question	Score
1. What is the extent of ease of the DevOps tools currently used in terms of supporting plug and play integrations? Check out if the tools support common DevOps plug-ins.	① ② ③ ④ ⑤
2. What is the extent of ease of integration of the tools being deployed currently, irrespective whether they are open source, commercial or in-house?	① ② ③ ④ ⑤
3. What is the extent to which the tools support full pipeline visibility? Do they enable orchestration and tracking of all releases at all stages planning, development, test and production including feedback loops and planning for the next release?	① ② ③ ④ ⑤
4. What is the extent to which continuous quality and shift-left testing are being executed through the DevOps toolchain and are being practiced in projects adopting DevOps? Check for testing being a continuous, regular and rigorous activity.	① ② ③ ④ ⑤

5.	What is the extent to which the toolchain helps in prioritize your testing and automate risk assessment for your releases?	① ② ③ ④ ⑤
6.	What is the extent to which the toolchain enables actionable analytics? Do you have a dashboard with meaningful metrics from pipeline operation to provide analytics that support real-time decisions, as well as inform improvements over time?	① ② ③ ④ ⑤
7.	What is the extent to which the toolchain enables you to get insights into release and pipeline performance, testing coverage and speed, release readiness, team productivity and so on?	① ② ③ ④ ⑤
8.	What is the extent to which the toolchain is orchestrated and aligned to deliver business value? In other words, does it provide intelligence about the app content in the pipeline? Can you see in the pipeline what code is deployed where and its status? Can you map how the content of a release aligns with business priorities?	① ② ③ ④ ⑤
9.	To what extent are all environments setup being created automatically from a single repository?	① ② ③ ④ ⑤

Leaders Think

Organizations that transform with DevOps are those that successfully embrace the DevOps mindset and adapt to the newer ways of working. But how do you make the new ways of working a business norm and reality? How do you build intergroup co-ordination and break the silos amongst multiple teams that have been working for ages side by side and still do not communicate enough? The answer lies in leveraging technology as an enabler and building enterprise toolchains leveraging existing enterprise tool stacks and designing a pipeline that facilitates such collaboration with the help of change agents and technical experts. Such toolchains are the cornerstones of a successful DevOps implementation and a critical success factor to achieve Continuous Quality with DevOps.

Umesh Jain, Vice President, Deutsche Bank Group

Continuous Integration

Continuous Integration (CI) is a key practice where developers integrate code into a source controlled shared repository frequently, preferably multiple times a day. Each integration is then verified by an automated build and automated tests.

Why Assess?

- Enables rapid feedback to correct defects as soon as they are introduced in the code base
- Enables automating the testing and building a document trail

Key Practice Summary

9
Practice
Continuous Integration
DevOps Discipline Mapping
*Organization Design for DevOps *CI-CD
Focus Groups
*Application Teams *Product Owners *Scrum Masters *Agile Coaches
Example Tools
*Jenkins *Git *Bamboo *Gradle *Docker *Kubernetes *Puppet Enterprise *Ansible *Apache Maven *TeamCity

Assessment Questions

**Questions to be scored on a scale of 1 to 5 (5 being ideal)*

***OSNA implies Objective Score Not Applicable*

Question		Score
1.	Are you using any source code repository?	**OSNA
2.	Are you using any tools for static code analysis?	**OSNA
3.	Are you using any build automation tools?	**OSNA
4.	Are you using any on-premise infrastructure or cloud-based infrastructure?	**OSNA
5.	Are you using scripts or orchestration tools to do application lifecycle management?	**OSNA
6.	To what extent are deployment pipelines configured as jobs using workflow plugins? Or are they configured otherwise?	① ② ③ ④ ⑤
7.	Does your CI tool have an operations center to audit for cluster operations? In case of production issues, how are these logs analyzed?	**OSNA
8.	What are the different stages in your pipeline? How do they map to jobs?	**OSNA
9.	To what extent is your pipeline designed for resiliency to failures?	① ② ③ ④ ⑤
10.	To what extent are checkpoint validations/triggers automated?	① ② ③ ④ ⑤
11.	What happens when a pipeline fails at any given stage?	**OSNA
12.	To what extent do you ensure your pre-production environments replicate the production environment?	① ② ③ ④ ⑤
13.	Have you established an audit trail using your CI tool (e.g., tools like Jenkins that have a plugin for audit trail)?	**OSNA
14.	In absence of audit trail, does your team maintain a job configuration history to examine the history of changes with change implementer and timestamp?	**OSNA
15.	How has your team established traceability using the tool (e.g., tools like Jenkins that use fingerprint to keep track of the artifacts)?	**OSNA
16.	How do you keep track of an artifact when it leaves the CI tool and gets deployed on a remote server? (Look out for mechanisms like deployment plugins available in Chef and Puppet)	**OSNA
17.	To what extent are your processes for compile, Unit testing, code quality checks standardized and complied with?	① ② ③ ④ ⑤

18. How is dependency management across components, environments, services and applications implemented in your project/program?	**OSNA
19. To what extent are gated checks defined and implemented in the CI pipeline?	① ② ③ ④ ⑤
20. To what extent do you have code quality checks integrated with the CI Tool?	① ② ③ ④ ⑤
21. To what extent are self-service and full nightly builds performed at least once daily?	① ② ③ ④ ⑤
22. To what extent are unit testing and functional testing integrated with the CI tool?	① ② ③ ④ ⑤
23. To what extent do you are your builds triggered through source control?	① ② ③ ④ ⑤
24. To what extent is notification enabled for build success status?	① ② ③ ④ ⑤
25. To what extent do you have a metrics dashboard for builds providing real-time build status and KPIs?	① ② ③ ④ ⑤

Leaders Think

Continuous Integration is a key practice that requires developers to check-in and integrate their source code into a shared repository multiple times a day. Every check-in executed is verified by an automated build enabling an early detection and notification of risks and problems to the entire team. It reduces the risk for every build and paves the path for faster delivery of business value.

Umesh Jain, Vice President, Deutsche Bank Group

Continuous Testing

Continuous Testing is a key practice that introduces automated test execution as an integral part of the DevOps pipeline and provides feedback on the business risks associated with the software at the earliest and real-time. It expects testing to be embedded as part of the development process and not a separate phase.

Why Assess?

Assessing this area is important for multiple reasons.

- Enables assessment of business risk coverage
- Tests each layer of modern architecture and enables actionable insights and feedback at every stage of the delivery pipeline
- Enables end-to-end testing to assess end-user experience across the technology stack
- Enables test optimization by minimizing redundancy in test suites
- Embraces the best of **shift-left** and **shift-right** testing paradigms

Key Practice Summary

10

Practice

Continuous Testing

DevOps Discipline Mapping

*Organization Design for DevOps
*CI-CD

Focus Groups

*Application Teams
*Technical Architects

Example Tools

*Jenkins
*Git
*Bamboo
*Gradle
*Docker
*Kubernetes
*Puppet Enterprise
*Ansible
*Apache Maven
*TeamCity

Assessment Questions

**Questions to be scored on a scale of 1 to 5 (5 being ideal)*

***OSNA implies Objective Score Not Applicable*

Question		Score
1.	To what extent is Continuous Testing integrated as a part of your DevOps Strategy?	1 2 3 4 5
2.	To what extent is Continuous Testing effective in assessing business risk coverage?	1 2 3 4 5
3.	To what extent is your automated testing providing critical insight and analytics that drive release decisions?	1 2 3 4 5
4.	To what extent have you shifted your testing efforts and focus to the API layer where feasible?	1 2 3 4 5
5.	To what extent do you use service virtualization and test data management to enable continuous testing?	1 2 3 4 5
6.	To what extent is functional testing integrated into the CI/CD pipeline?	1 2 3 4 5
7.	Are you using automation tools to perform load testing, functional testing, mobile testing and security testing?	**OSNA
8.	What are the tools and frameworks deployed to ensure continuous testing?	**OSNA
9.	To what extent are the delivery audits performed and audit results visible to the release manager for Go /No-Go /Conditional-Go decisions?	1 2 3 4 5
10.	To what extent are the teams performing test and defect management using tools?	1 2 3 4 5
11.	To what extent are test cases written along with requirements/user stories?	1 2 3 4 5
12.	To what extent are necessary dedicated test environments made available as needed?	1 2 3 4 5
13.	To what extent is there a clear traceability between Defect Management and build and release?	1 2 3 4 5
14.	To what extent are testing metrics defined and collected?	1 2 3 4 5
15.	To what extent is manual unit testing with coverage defined as per policy guidelines from customer/organization?	1 2 3 4 5
16.	To what extent are notifications implemented for testing feedback?	1 2 3 4 5
17.	To what extent is performance testing performed using tools?	1 2 3 4 5

18.	To what extent are the teams using security testing tools?	1	2	3	4	5
19.	To what extent does the build verification test (smoke test) happen for every build?	1	2	3	4	5
20.	To what extent are service virtualization technologies implemented?	1	2	3	4	5
21.	To what extent are multiple test environment configurations available within 30 - 60 mins?	1	2	3	4	5
22.	To what extent are practices like BDD (behaviour-driven development) implemented?	1	2	3	4	5
23.	To what extent are tools available for synthetic data generation and test environment management?	1	2	3	4	5
24.	To what extent is functional testing automated and integrated in the continuous integration pipeline on each commit?	1	2	3	4	5
25.	To what extent is test data management and maintenance integrated as part of your DevOps strategy and is being implemented?	1	2	3	4	5
26.	To what extent is the non-functional testing automated?	1	2	3	4	5
27.	To what extent is automated unit testing achieving significant coverage?	1	2	3	4	5
28.	To what extent is the user acceptance testing automated?	1	2	3	4	5

Leaders Think

In today's world, the informed customers demand seamless user experience; the solutions built to provide this need an extraordinary connectivity and dependencies amongst processes, systems and infrastructure. In short, these solutions - applications, products, services can become very complex and can pose big challenge as testing needs to ensure that high quality software is delivered at a fast-track speed; and this is where Continuous Testing in a DevOps culture plays a crucial role. Continuous testing needs automated end-to-end testing solutions that integrate existing development processes while excluding errors and enabling continuity throughout SDLC. Bringing in a DevOps culture helps erase the boundaries of various roles in the SDLC process and make sure everyone contributes across the value chain to maximize Quality of end product.

Atulya Pradhan, Transformation Champion, Capgemini

Continuous Monitoring

Continuous monitoring is a key practice that enables risk or issue detection associated with application performance in production and pre-production environments.

Why Assess?

Assessing this area is important for multiple reasons.

- Enables performance management of applications, services and systems in production environments to continuously scan for risks, issues and errors in applications hosted both on prem and on cloud
- Enables real-time logging of errors and exceptions
- Enables monitoring the health, uptime and performance of the available hardware resources like servers
- Enables exposing vulnerabilities in the application code and less secure coding practices and third-party software integration
- Enables setup of failed builds and deployments
- Enables user activity monitoring that helps teams drive feature development and infrastructure scaling needs

Key Practice Summary

11
Practice
Continuous Monitoring
DevOps Discipline Mapping
*Organization Design for DevOps *Continuous Monitoring
Focus Groups
*Application Teams *Technical Architects
Example Tools
*Nagios *ELK (Elastisearch, Logstash, Kibana) *Consul.io *Jenkins *Splunk *Appdynamics *trust.salesforce.com APIs *Grafana *Riemann *Zebbix *Zennos

Assessment Questions

**Questions to be scored on a scale of 1 to 5 (5 being ideal)*

***OSNA implies Objective Score Not Applicable*

Question	Score
1. Are you using any tools for application and infrastructure monitoring?	**OSNA
2. How do you ensure stability of complex codebases? (Look out for small releases and frequent deployment and monitoring)	**OSNA
3. To what extent do your monitoring solutions troubleshoot application errors, data bottlenecks, user issues and other infrastructure problems?	① ② ③ ④ ⑤
4. To what extent do your monitoring solutions exhibit cross-platform versatility?	① ② ③ ④ ⑤
5. To what extent do your monitoring solutions eliminate silo thinking and tune your applications and infrastructure to operate in seamless unison?	① ② ③ ④ ⑤

6.	To what extent do your monitoring solutions combine performance data from multiple sources of truth into a logical single source of truth that can be leveraged as actionable analytics?	① ② ③ ④ ⑤
7.	To what extent are your tool generated reports visible to and consumed by different stakeholders without extensive customization?	① ② ③ ④ ⑤
8.	To what extent do you have performance monitoring tools implemented to give reports of application performance?	① ② ③ ④ ⑤
9.	To what extent do you have application and infrastructure monitoring implemented across environments?	① ② ③ ④ ⑤
10.	To what extent are log collection, investigation, troubleshooting, normalization and categorization in place?	① ② ③ ④ ⑤
11.	To what extent are there dashboards for log reporting and log analytics?	① ② ③ ④ ⑤
12.	To what extent do you have a reporting mechanism in place for getting integrated reports from the DevOps tools?	① ② ③ ④ ⑤
13.	Have you implemented any tools for pattern detection?	**OSNA
14.	Are you able to have anomaly detection by running dynamic queries?	**OSNA
15.	Do you have a single view dashboard defined that covers all activities within the delivery pipeline?	**OSNA
16.	To what extent do you have historical and real-time, crossfunction reports available and visible to all stakeholders?	① ② ③ ④ ⑤
17.	To what extent do you have cross-function report trending available and leveraged for analysis?	① ② ③ ④ ⑤
18.	To what extent do you have a continuous improvement process based on the metrics from monitoring?	① ② ③ ④ ⑤

Leaders Think

Continuous Monitoring is a practice that enables an enterprise find holes in its financial and operational environment that comprises of people, process, tools, technologies, systems and infrastructure. It enables automated analysis of all event and transaction data using logs and enables pattern recognition for any kind of risks or malicious events that need special attention and remediation. Thus, it is a critical element of risk management in any organization.

Amit Naidu, Technical Program Lead, Wolterskluwer

Telemetry

Telemetry is a practice that enables us to automatically collect data about product usage, customer engagement and actionable analytics from actual customer usage. It differs from logging in the sense that logging is more about diagnosing errors with code, whereas telemetry is procuring insights post product deployment. Also, logging is a function that procures data internally, whereas telemetry procures data from external customers.

Why Assess?

Assessing this area is important for multiple reasons.

- It enables an end user to monitor the state of an object or environment while remote
- Telemetry dashboard insights provide value to decision making, performance monitoring and management
- Analytics procured can be leveraged to prioritize release updates
- Enables finding out customer expectations about features and their engagement with the product
- Enables finding out crash analytics with trends on crash frequencies and context

Key Practice Summary

Assessment Questions

**Questions to be scored on a scale of 1 to 5 (5 being ideal)*

***OSNA implies Objective Score Not Applicable*

Question		Score
1.	To what extent have the measures around telemetry been successful in improving the predictability around build failures? Look for examples and trends.	1 2 3 4 5
2.	To what extent do your Telemetry mechanisms monitor for both audit and compliance issues and act as a preventive mechanism for security breaches? Look for examples and trends.	1 2 3 4 5
3.	To what extent do you monitor production issues and outages to see and solve problems as they occur? Look for examples and trends.	1 2 3 4 5
4.	To what extent do you monitor user behaviour to get product feedback? Look for examples and trends.	1 2 3 4 5

Leaders Think

With an increasing number of enterprises adopting DevOps, integrating telemetry with application development has become an imperative for all forward-thinking practitioners. But access to a multitude of tools with the same purpose residing in the organization makes it difficult to organize and standardize an end to end enterprise tool suite. Incorporating telemetry to simplify enterprise tooling prevents such problems and enables developers leverage technology and feature analytics to mitigate application risks and challenges. Telemetry enables you to record system Behaviour. To ensure that you incorporate telemetry into design, your pre-production and production environments as well as your deployment pipeline should be a replica of each other and generate datapoints for telemetry continuously. Whenever, an incident or a problem occurs, you will be able to interpret it quickly and take corrective actions viewing the telemetry records.

Umesh Jain, Vice President, Deutsche Bank Group

Continuous Delivery and Deployment

Continuous Delivery (CD) is the next step to continuous integration. It enables automating the entire release workflow. It aims to make the release deliverable with application of business rules as appropriate. It still requires a person or business rule to decide when the final push to production should be executed. Continuous Deployment is a further advancement of continuous delivery. It facilitates code deployment into production without any human intervention.

Why Assess?

- Enables fully scripted deployments that are more consistent, accurate, repeatable and error-free
- Enables shorter release deployment cycles and more stable releases

Key Practice Summary

13
Practice
Continuous Delivery and Deployment
DevOps Discipline Mapping
*Organization Design for DevOps *CI-CD
Focus Groups
*Application Teams *Technical Architects
Example Inputs
*Jenkins *ElectricFlow *Microsoft Visual Studio *Octopus Deploy *IBM Urban Code *AWS Code Deploy *DeployBot *Shippable *ElasticBox *CA Automic *Go CD *Electric Cloud

Assessment Questions

**Questions to be scored on a scale of 1 to 5 (5 being ideal)*

***OSNA implies Objective Score Not Applicable*

Question	Score
1. To what extent are you using automated scripts in production and non-production environments in order to deploy applications?	① ② ③ ④ ⑤
2. Which tool(s) are being used to orchestrate the deployment pipeline?	**OSNA
3. To what extent can you deploy simultaneously the same components to all environments automatically?	① ② ③ ④ ⑤
4. To what extent are there mechanisms in place to assess production readiness to deploy the code? Look out for mechanisms.	① ② ③ ④ ⑤
5. To what extent are your deployments fully scripted?	① ② ③ ④ ⑤
6. To what extent is your environment provisioning fully scripted?	① ② ③ ④ ⑤
7. To what extent are your build artifacts not environment specific?	① ② ③ ④ ⑤
8. To what extent are standard environment provisioning and deployment processes defined and implemented?	① ② ③ ④ ⑤
9. To what extent are there push button deployments to test environments being executed?	① ② ③ ④ ⑤
10. To what extent are notifications and logging configured in deployment workflow?	① ② ③ ④ ⑤
11. To what extent are there standardized common deployment scripts and across all environments?	① ② ③ ④ ⑤
12. To what extent are there push button deployments to pre-prod environment executed?	① ② ③ ④ ⑤
13. To what extent do you have an automated provisioning and deployment of the database?	① ② ③ ④ ⑤
14. To what extent are there push button deployments to production environment being executed?	① ② ③ ④ ⑤
15. To what extent do you have coordinated, multi-tier orchestrated deployments (governance with workflow)?	① ② ③ ④ ⑤
16. To what extent do you promote VM or Container for deployments?	① ② ③ ④ ⑤
17. To what extent do you have zero touch deployment up to production?	① ② ③ ④ ⑤

18.	To what extent do you have built-in capabilities to rollback to any of your previous code versions in any of your environments?	(1) (2) (3) (4) (5)
19.	To what extent are all pre-productive environments integrated into the continuous deployment schedule?	(1) (2) (3) (4) (5)

Leaders Think

Most organizations are embracing DevOps to shorten their release cycle times to production and enhance their time to market. New features are being added to existing legacy systems leveraging the principles of microservices architecture. Leveraging the agility promised by microservices requires a strong foundation of continuous integration, delivery and continuous deployment. Irrespective of the target deployment environment, a robust Continuous Delivery and Deployment workflow is needed to get changes to software rolled out to production.

Amit Naidu, Technical Program Lead, Wolterskluwer

Infrastructure

Infrastructure

Role of Infrastructure in a DevOps Transformation

When organizations move to the cloud, security models also change and identity-based security protocols and technologies become a key imperative. Infrastructure setup, scaling up and security needs, therefore, play an important role in the overall DevOps transformation of an enterprise and should be integrated with the overall DevOps strategy.

Assessment Objectives

- Enables detailed recommendations on migrating to newer variants in infrastructure based on business objectives, technical landscape and strategic priorities for new applications
- Enables a view of risks, improvement areas and action items that impact performance and scalability of existing or planned web applications from a current and future state migration to cloud perspective

Key Practices Summary

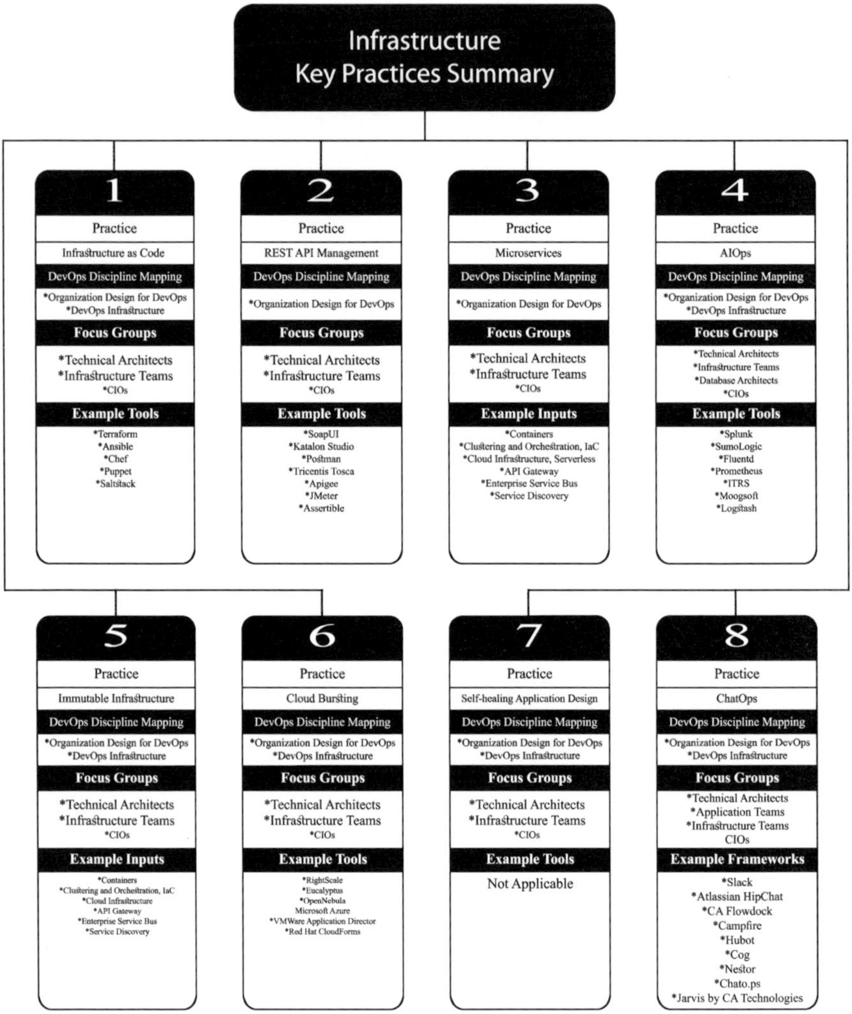

Infrastructure as Code

Infrastructure as Code (IaC) is programmable infrastructure. It is a practice that allows developers to configure environments and provision the technology stack using automated scripts as opposed to the traditional manual process of configuring different operating systems and hardware devices.

Why Assess?

- Enables more versatility and adaptability in infrastructure provisioning and deployment reducing the cost of shadow IT support
- Enables source control management and compliance with design practices for infrastructure and improves site reliability
- Code-based automation allows developers to control source code configurations, test iteratively and release the software only when rigorously tested and production ready
- Enables a faster response to new IT requirements with better site reliability, security and compliance with the organization's IT and security standards
- Better Customer Satisfaction through higher quality of service delivered within shorter delivery times
- Reduced OPEX through reliable infrastructure deployed in minutes saving on people costs and mitigating security-related financial risks
- Reduced CAPEX by enabling self-reliance in developers and testers to address the infrastructure needs for their projects and programs in the context of DevOps
- Standardization of infrastructure configurations improves reliability and flexibility to autoscale dynamically with minimum waste of resources based on business needs or roll back if a change fails
- Enables an on-demand computing resources pool with reduced manual overhead

Key Practice Summary

1
Practice
Infrastructure as Code
DevOps Discipline Mapping
*Organization Design for DevOps *DevOps Infrastructure
Focus Groups
*Technical Architects *Infrastructure Teams *CIOs
Example Tools
*Terraform *Ansible *Chef *Puppet *Saltstack

Assessment Questions

**Questions to be scored on a scale of 1 to 5 (5 being ideal)*

***OSNA implies Objective Score Not Applicable*

Question		Score
1.	To what extent is IaC integrated with your organization's DevOps Strategy?	1 2 3 4 5
2.	How is infrastructure configured and managed?	**OSNA
3.	For larger programs, how is infrastructure as a code deployed?	**OSNA
4.	To what extent do you ensure that there is no configuration drift in IaC that can result in potential unintended service failures?	1 2 3 4 5
5.	To what extent do you ensure that IaC does not lead to accidental destruction in steady state? Look at examples of steady state issues caused due to IaC if any.	1 2 3 4 5
6.	To what extent does IaC ensure automated and error-free service provisioning?	1 2 3 4 5

7.	To what extent do you ensure a foolproof auditing mechanism in place for IaC? In other words, how do you ensure that any human errors in the initial piece of code for infrastructure that creates multiple machines as replication are corrected for every instance? Look out for actual instances.	(1) (2) (3) (4) (5)
8.	To what extent is the skill gap for transitioning to the IaC handled through training and on-the-job learning to create a competent and capable team?	(1) (2) (3) (4) (5)
9.	To what extent do you have a well-defined IT Landscape and application architecture at the organization level that allows you to define implementation, configuration and operation of IaC tools?	(1) (2) (3) (4) (5)

Leaders Think

Infrastructure as Code is nothing but automation of your entire environmental infrastructure. Initially there was lot of challenge configuring environments for cloud. Technology address this gap with providing JSON based templates that allow you to write code and configure environments consistently with scripts. So, when the job runs, it picks up the JSON code from JSON file and as per the code, it starts provisioning resources in the cloud or on on-premise data center. Thus said, infrastructure as code helps you automate your environment provisioning process and once this is done, you can put your CI/CD process on top of it to run containerized architectures in the most secure and efficient manner.

Anil Kumar, Solution Director, HCL Technologies

REST API Management

REST API management is the process of overseeing RESTful application programming interfaces (REST APIs) in a secure, scalable environment

Why Assess?

Security is of the utmost importance when companies are exposing their backend systems by way of APIs. This is the primary reason why any enterprise needs to consider API management is to secure their APIs. They provide reports and dashboards that give both operations and businesses a panoramic look at their digital business. Thanks to API monetization, you are able to start charging for revenue shares, usage, as well as to keep track of all billing and payments in real-time.

Key Practice Summary

2
Practice
REST API Management
DevOps Discipline Mapping
*Organization Design for DevOps
Focus Groups
*Technical Architects *Infrastructure Teams *CIOs
Example Tools
*SoapUI *Katalon Studio *Postman *Tricentis Tosca *Apigee *JMeter *Assertible

Assessment Questions

**Questions to be scored on a scale of 1 to 5 (5 being ideal)*

***OSNA implies Objective Score Not Applicable*

Question		Score
1.	To what extent can teams define and manage requirements and present them in a structured and visual way that everyone in the software development lifecycle can understand?	① ② ③ ④ ⑤
2.	How is requirements prioritization and scaling engineered across teams and projects?	**OSNA
3.	Do you have a central artifact repository for storing all the requirements and are all changes managed in an autonomous manner?	**OSNA
4.	To what extent do you have a centralized solution to help teams develop, test and securely publish APIs, making them available for developer and app consumption?	① ② ③ ④ ⑤
5.	What is the available solution for API development, testing, publishing and discovery?	**OSNA
6.	Is this solution available for all capabilities or only a few?	**OSNA
7.	To what extent is this a centralized solution that enables teams to develop, test, secure and publish APIs to enable developer discovery and onboarding?	① ② ③ ④ ⑤
8.	To what extent can you manage the full lifecycle of your APIs and understand API program performance?	① ② ③ ④ ⑤
9.	To what extent have you implemented open tracing using vendor-neutral APIs and instrumentation for distributed tracing?	① ② ③ ④ ⑤
10.	To what extent do your current security policies and mechanisms ensure blocking attacks through REST APIs, ensuring sensitive data is not accidentally or intentionally leaked?	① ② ③ ④ ⑤

Leaders Think

Most organizations are shifting to microservices architecture for developing newer services or features to their existing applications. Consumption of microservices in a secure manner requires that its exposed functionality has secure APIs with no risk of accidental or intentional data leakage through any form of security breaches. A robust API management practice also provides techniques to detect or prevent such cyberattacks.

Umesh Jain, Vice President, Deutsche Bank Group

Microservices

Microservices are independently scalable application components that are loosely coupled, tightly scoped and independently deployable as services. They support the scaling of existing applications leveraging team agility and DevOps practices for development.

Why Assess?

- Microservices give you more control over the impact of changes to the environment
- They enable faster development of new features without changing and retesting the entire monolithic application for each feature, thus providing increased development throughput
- They enable feature deployment several times a day to live production as well as support high web traffic volumes
- They provide scalability, cloud readiness and implementation technology flexibility, all of which together reduce the total cost of ownership

Key Practice Summary

3
Practice
Microservices
DevOps Discipline Mapping
*Organization Design for DevOps
Focus Groups
*Technical Architects *Infrastructure Teams *CIOs
Example Inputs
*Containers *Clustering and Orchestration, IaC *Cloud Infrastructure, Serverless *API Gateway *Enterprise Service Bus *Service Discovery

Assessment Questions

**Questions to be scored on a scale of 1 to 5 (5 being ideal)*

***OSNA implies Objective Score Not Applicable*

Question		Score
1.	To what extent is the system architected to deliver continuous value to your customers?	① ② ③ ④ ⑤
2.	To what extent are newer services built around the monolithic architecture using microservices for decoupling the system architecture? In case not, what is the approach followed?	① ② ③ ④ ⑤
3.	To what extent in the case of microservices architecture being leveraged for new components is functional cohesion achieved?	① ② ③ ④ ⑤
4.	To what extent is the enterprise architecture tightly coupled overall?	① ② ③ ④ ⑤
5.	To what extent are the 12-factor application design principles applied for all microservices developed?	① ② ③ ④ ⑤
6.	To what extent are your applications or services suitable for deployment on modern cloud platforms with minimum system administration needs?	① ② ③ ④ ⑤
7.	To what extent does your microservices design externalize storage-related activities to explicit persistency services so that these tasks can be limited to the services that deal with persistence? And how do you verify that the backup and archive is consistent and usable?	① ② ③ ④ ⑤
8.	To what extent are recovery point objectives (RPO) met by your backups and archival process?	① ② ③ ④ ⑤
9.	To what extent are recovery time objectives (RTO) met by your backups and archival process?	① ② ③ ④ ⑤
10.	To what extent are your microservices designed with health check APIs that facilitate the best check of their critical resources and workflows?	① ② ③ ④ ⑤
11.	What is the predictability that changes in architecture will not result in unexpected breaks in architecture elsewhere?	① ② ③ ④ ⑤

Leaders Think

Microservices are an architectural pattern where you break your bigger functionality into smaller functionalities and develop your components, APIs, etc. around it. These have their own database, their own APIs for exposing feature functionality to the external world. By design and default, the microservices architecture supports domain driven design. On the technical implementation perspective, microservices can ease the development effort along with a flexibility to individually scale up or down. So, it creates a complete isolation around the service or functionality and any changes or defects can be fixed independently without pulling the entire application down. As against this, with a monolithic architecture, even a small change requires retesting of the entire application with all other components where the component in scope of change has been referenced.

Shifting to a microservices architecture enables faster deployment of changes to production in small and independent releases with decentralized governance. However, it may be also important to have a repository of all services that are being moved to microservices architecture with bounded contexts and loose coupling. With more and more organizations adopting DevOps in the digital era today, microservices are defining the building blocks of enterprise architecture.

Anil Kumar, Solution Director, HCL Technologies

AIOps

AIOps is a key practice that facilitates AI and machine learning to enhance, complement or optimize a broad range of IT operations, resulting in a more efficient and predictive insight driven environment.

Why Assess?

The primary objective to assess this area is to discover patterns to describe databases being considered and leverage that for real-time and historical analysis to predict possible future incidents.

Key Practice Summary

4
Practice
AIOps
DevOps Discipline Mapping
*Organization Design for DevOps *DevOps Infrastructure
Focus Groups
*Technical Architects *Infrastructure Teams *Database Architects *CIOs
Example Tools
*Splunk *SumoLogic *Fluentd *Prometheus *ITRS *Moogsoft *Logstash

Assessment Questions

**Questions to be scored on a scale of 1 to 5 (5 being ideal)*

***OSNA implies Objective Score Not Applicable*

Question		Score
1.	To what extent are AIOps and machine learning integrated into your DevOps Strategy?	1 2 3 4 5
2.	To what extent does AIOps make the daily tasks of DevOps engineers simpler?	1 2 3 4 5
3.	To what extent does AIOps facilitate removal of data silos and root-cause remediation?	1 2 3 4 5
4.	To what extent does AIOps facilitate better collaboration and enable evaluation of business strategies?	1 2 3 4 5
5.	To what extent does AIOps facilitate performance optimization?	1 2 3 4 5
6.	To what extent is AIOps applied to IT operations as a part of your strategy?	1 2 3 4 5
7.	To what extent are AIOps and machine learning applied to monitoring, operations, infrastructure data and help desk automation?	1 2 3 4 5
8.	To what extent does AIOps enable high availability and reliability of application infrastructure?	1 2 3 4 5

Leaders Think

The Artificial intelligence for IT operation is called AIOps. AIOps is the NextGen and future of IT operation. AIOps integrates advance algorithms and AI for analyzing the raw data from the numerous sources and provides meaningful information to speed service delivery, increase IT efficiency and delivers an exceptional user experience.

So, the question arises as to where does AIOps fit into IT environment? Looking at AIOps and hearing integration of complex algorithms and advance analytics with IT, confuses and creates curiosity how this will fit into overall modern IT tools landscape. Will it really replace the existing monitoring, log management, service desk orchestration tools and the entire support staff? The answer is No. The objective of AIOps is not to replace the existing IT tool landscape, but rather complement and sit on the top of the existing infrastructure to consume the data and provide useful real-time information to its users. The objective is to empower ITOps to drive business for the 21st century by leveraging cutting edging technology. Going forward, AIOps will play a key role in enabling new efficiency for IT Ops teams. It will also make practical the adoption of complex next-generation technologies that cannot be managed successfully using traditional solutions.

Madan Upadhyay, CEO and Founder, Emergen Teck

Immutable Infrastructure

Immutable infrastructure is a software management strategy that involves destroying and replacing each instance of an application or service when the application or service needs to be updated. It is made of immutable components that are replaced for every deployment, rather than being updated in-place.

Why Assess?

This approach is different from traditional software management because, under the immutable infrastructure model, changes are not made to software that is live and running. Immutable infrastructure helps to lower the risk of introducing accidental configuration changes that could lead to security problems. It also minimizes "configuration drift," or the tendency of configurations of similar platforms to diverge over time and therefore become harder to manage.

Finally, it reduces the chance that a configuration change to a running instance will cause the instance to fail and lead to service disruptions. With immutable infrastructure, changes can be tested thoroughly before they are brought live through a new instance. It is also easy to revert to an earlier configuration if something goes wrong when a new instance goes live.

Why are containers popular towards Immutable Infrastructure?

Containers are a popular building block for immutable infrastructure because containers make it possible to create multiple instances of an application or service based on container images. When updates need to be applied to the application or service, the container image is updated and new container instances are spun up in place of the old ones. There is no need to reconfigure the application or service instances while they are running and updates can be thoroughly vetted before the new instance is launched.

Key Benefits of Immutable Infrastructure

- Immutable infrastructure will complement continuous integration and DevOps quite well
- It gets rid of the complications of needing to track the fine differences in tons of system images that the virtual infrastructure uses.
- Facilitates smaller codebases and greater modularity in architecture
- Enables an order of magnitude speedup of workload start-up, thereby enabling greater agility in the development process
- Enables environment standardization
- Promotes efficient resource utilization

Key Practice Summary

5

Practice

Immutable Infrastructure

DevOps Discipline Mapping

*Organization Design for DevOps
*DevOps Infrastructure

Focus Groups

*Technical Architects
*Infrastructure Teams
*CIOs

Example Inputs

*Containers
*Clustering and Orchestration, IaC
*Cloud Infrastructure
*API Gateway
*Enterprise Service Bus
*Service Discovery

Assessment Questions

**Questions to be scored on a scale of 1 to 5 (5 being ideal)*

***OSNA implies Objective Score Not Applicable*

Question		Score
1.	To what extent are your containers integrated within your corporate security and compliance framework? Check how smooth is this integration.	1 2 3 4 5
2.	To what extent do your containers support hybrid infrastructure?	1 2 3 4 5
3.	To what extent do your application-centric container management services (Container as a Service) enable customers to choose between application deployments in the data center or public cloud?	1 2 3 4 5
4.	To what extent do you have an infrastructure suitable to our vision and to bolster your future use cases?	1 2 3 4 5
5.	To what extent are your containers managed in alignment with the principles of declarative container management?	1 2 3 4 5
6.	To what extent do you have business cases clearly defined for every application being containerized?	1 2 3 4 5
7.	How are clusters and containers within clusters orchestrated?	**OSNA
8.	Do you have in place a data management organization?	**OSNA

Leaders Think

Immutable Infrastructure is the idea of using virtualized or containerized environments that are created once, used for a period of time and replaced since a change to the environment is required. The running infrastructure is never modified, just replaced be a new version. This way you can turn off all access to the infrastructure that isn't doing it's job and all output is item service responses, log messages or data updates. This limits the attack surface of the infrastructure.

Thomas Stiehm, CTO, Coveros, Inc.

Immutable infrastructure is becoming the norm of most organizations going digital today. It essentially makes your deployment workflows more consistent, reliable and predictable preventing popular issues like snowflake servers and configuration drift that occur with mutable infrastructures.

Umesh Jain, Vice President, Deutsche Bank Group

Cloud Bursting

Cloud bursting is a model for application deployment that promotes flexibility and optimal cost to an organization. Using cloud bursting, an application runs in either a private data center or cloud and when there is spike in demand for higher capacity of computational resources, it bursts into a public cloud. The key benefit of this hybrid cloud deployment model is that an organization does not need to maintain infrastructure all through the year to meet surge capacities, only pays for extra compute resources when they are needed and does not spend huge amounts forecasting specific peaks and surges in demand for infrastructure and computing power.

Why Assess?

- Leveraging cloud bursting appropriately and securely gives flexibility, scalability and cost savings from infrastructure and total cost of ownership.
- It allows switching of workloads on demand from on-prem private cloud to public cloud infrastructure.
- Enables enterprises to place their dev-test workloads into the public cloud while retaining their application databases and key servers and services on premise.
- Enables cloud migration of legacy applications without any major re architecting of the data center and application architecture.

Key Practice Summary

6
Practice
Cloud Bursting
DevOps Discipline Mapping
*Organization Design for DevOps *DevOps Infrastructure
Focus Groups
*Technical Architects *Infrastructure Teams *CIOs
Example Tools
*RightScale *Eucalyptus *OpenNebula Microsoft Azure *VMWare Application Director *Red Hat CloudForms

Assessment Questions

**Questions to be scored on a scale of 1 to 5 (5 being ideal)*

***OSNA implies Objective Score Not Applicable*

Question	Score
1. Are you able to automatically increase the scale to deal with a large traffic event?	**OSNA
2. Are you able to reduce this scale back down in order to save on expenditures?	**OSNA
3. Does your infrastructure include redundancies?	**OSNA
4. Is your stack able to deal with failures in the availability zone, application, VM and the process level?	**OSNA
5. How do you monitor and manage the health of your services?	**OSNA
6. To what extent does your cloud bursting strategy enable you to optimize distribution and redundancy in order to reduce downtime as much as possible throughout the operation, upgrades to the platform and updates to security?	① ② ③ ④ ⑤
7. To what extent do you consider security and compliance requirements with cloud bursting in a hybrid cloud environment?	① ② ③ ④ ⑤
8. To what extent do you consider latency, load balancing and platform compatibility with cloud bursting in a hybrid cloud environment?	① ② ③ ④ ⑤

9.	To what extent is your sensitive data de-risked (from bursting it in a public cloud) and environment compliant with standards like PCI-DSS with your current strategy for cloud bursting?	① ② ③ ④ ⑤
10.	To what extent have you achieved infrastructure and environment compatibility that are needed to make cloud bursting happen?	① ② ③ ④ ⑤
11.	To what extent do your cloud service providers and virtualization vendors manage hybrid environments using the same platform?	① ② ③ ④ ⑤
12.	To what extent are the pipelines which you use declarative (in terms of coding) for ease of version control, remediation and tracebility?	① ② ③ ④ ⑤
13.	How is your road to production looking right now? What is blocking your way and what inefficiencies are holding you back?	**OSNA

Leaders Think

Cloud Bursting is the application of a hybrid cloud deployment strategy where applications that normally run in a private cloud may use a public cloud to handle peak times or incidents where private cloud resources don't meet the needs of the application. From a security POV you need to design your applications to be able to transfer data securely between the private and public resources. It might also include special provisions for how the data is processed and stored in the public cloud that might not be needed if you were only going to run the workload in a private cloud.

Thomas Stiehm, CTO, Coveros, Inc.

Cloud bursting is an application deployment practice that enables leverage the best of private and public cloud computing capacity. For surge capacities that are one time demands, an organization need not maintain a continuous fixed capacity equal to the surge demand as it would be otherwise a very high cost for all infrastructure resources. Typically, under spikes, basic applications are moved to public cloud with a pay-per-use pricing model and business critical applications gain access to local resources improving overall efficiency. Compliance and security requirements, load balancing, latency and platform compatibility are key factors to consider while leveraging cloud bursting for optimal efficiency.

Umesh Jain, Vice President, Deutsche Bank Group

Self-healing Application Design

Applications and services today ever evolving and certainly break or fail at some point or the other. With distributed systems commonly in place, hardware or network failures are equally common. All such failures and disruptions need to be planned for to the extent possible. How do we factor all such factors at the time of application design itself so that the applications self-heal or auto-correct themselves at such times? How do they develop resiliency from failures and become more predictable and stable? That's precisely the objective of self-healing application design.

Why Assess?

- Self-healing applications make the system highly reliable by having a minimal downtime and auto-correcting failures
- Facilitates zero intervention production

Key Practice Summary

7
Practice
Self-healing Application Design
DevOps Discipline Mapping
*Organization Design for DevOps *DevOps Infrastructure
Focus Groups
*Technical Architects *Infrastructure Teams *CIOs
Example Tools
Not Applicable

Assessment Questions

**Questions to be scored on a scale of 1 to 5 (5 being ideal)*

***OSNA implies Objective Score Not Applicable*

Question	Score
1. To what extent do the autoscaling mechanisms for your application also take into account the dependencies for autoscaling components dependent on them?	① ② ③ ④ ⑤
2. To what extent are the troubleshooting principles for redeploying resources and application components effective?	① ② ③ ④ ⑤
3. To what extent is the availability of resiliency features for each application identified and established for every location?	① ② ③ ④ ⑤
4. To what extent are the resiliency features integrated into a centralized service so that they can be available in locations where they are not available?	① ② ③ ④ ⑤
5. To what extent are the application's self-healing capabilities for automatic recovery initiation and time required for self-healing considered to be successful?	① ② ③ ④ ⑤
6. To what extent do you have central monitoring systems that can track which clouds autoscale resources and which clouds don't?	① ② ③ ④ ⑤
7. To what extent do you have scale schedules defined and coordinated for optimal scaling?	① ② ③ ④ ⑤
8. To what extent do the self-healing mechanisms for all high availability applications ensure zero intervention production?	① ② ③ ④ ⑤
9. To what extent are all business-critical systems protected by appropriate high availability solutions?	① ② ③ ④ ⑤
10. To what extent do all the business-critical systems have disaster recovery capability?	① ② ③ ④ ⑤
11. For any of the business-critical applications, is any of the infrastructure a potential single point of failure?	**OSNA

Leaders Think

Self-healing application design focusses on failure detection, graceful response to failures and logging and monitoring of failures to give operational insight. Response design for specific type of failures may also depend upon an application's availability requirements. For instance, an application that is business critical and demands very high availability may switch to a secondary region in case of complete outage. This would be at an expense of costs as compared to a single region deployment. Data centers are most commonly designed with fail-over instructions to ensure automated business continuity of operations.

Umesh Jain, Vice President, Deutsche Bank Group

ChatOps

ChatOps (a marriage made between Chatbot and operations) is a practice that facilitates conversation driven development using tools blurring silos, integrating teams and bringing people together. It is a way of automating tasks by intelligent, conversational, natural language interface. It is about leveraging Chatbot just like team members to execute through custom scripts and plugins that can facilitate deployments, notifications or event responses for software security.

It enables automation to connect people, processes and tools in a way that drives transparency in the DevOps pipeline and promotes collaboration. It injects conversation directly in the middle of individual and interaction.

Why Assess?

- Aims at reducing organizational friction by bringing teams together.
- Enables a culture of DIY (Do It Yourself) or self-service. It empowers the people to put them in the charge of helping themselves.
- Improves problem solving efficiency and incident resolution rates due to higher team collaboration, automating common queries, repetitive manual activities and bridging the delayed communication.
- Enables real-time continuous monitoring of deployment pipeline and production systems results in improved problem management overall.

Key Practice Summary

8
Practice
ChatOps
DevOps Discipline Mapping
*Organization Design for DevOps *DevOps Infrastructure
Focus Groups
*Technical Architects *Application Teams *Infrastructure Teams CIOs
Example Frameworks
*Slack *Atlassian HipChat *CA Flowdock *Campfire *Hubot *Cog *Nestor *Chato.ps *Jarvis by CA Technologies

Assessment Questions

**Questions to be scored on a scale of 1 to 5 (5 being ideal)*

***OSNA implies Objective Score Not Applicable*

Question	Score
1. To what extent is ChatOps integrated as part of your overall DevOps Strategy?	① ② ③ ④ ⑤
2. To what extent does ChatOps facilitate rapid organizational learning?	① ② ③ ④ ⑤
3. To what extent does ChatOps help facilitate open communication within your distributed teams?	① ② ③ ④ ⑤
4. To what extent are Chatbots integrated with your Deployment Pipeline so as to automatically trigger notifications, share status and integrate intelligence in day to day delivery decisions?	① ② ③ ④ ⑤
5. To what extent are your Chatbots integrated with Incident Recording Systems as well as liaised with upstream and downstream applications and customer-facing teams?	① ② ③ ④ ⑤
6. To what extent are your Chatbots designed and operational to create smart alerts that require no follow-ups?	① ② ③ ④ ⑤

7.	To what extent are Chatbot based escalations effective and correct?	① ② ③ ④ ⑤
8.	To what extent are your workflows for managing incidents, escalations and deploying code all triggered using Chatbots?	① ② ③ ④ ⑤

Leaders Think

In today's volatile world, business is trying to do more with less by leveraging automation and DevOps is no more exception in the game. At the heart of DevOps, the goal is to foster better communication and collaboration between development and operation team. DevOps mainly aims to deploy features in the production faster, detect the problem quickly and ensure highly availability of the services.

Now with the advent of Artificial intelligence has open the doors for conversational bots i.e. Chatbot that is ready to change the game of business conversation. Chatbot is a solution that enables a conversation with end customers just like a human.

Let me cite what I mean here with some example use cases.

1. **Support** – The business can use bots in support to respond to the users query. They can be used in some conversation with the stakeholders.

   Developer to Siri – "What is the status of build #21985?"

   Siri to Developer – "It's under progress on QA environment. I will notify you once deployment is done. Please find the attach logs and screen shot for your reference."

2. **CI/CD** – Getting more information by tests, builds and deployments without engaging Ops.

   Siri to Developer – "development pipeline is broken with test case #21349, please fix it immediately to promote the code to next environment."

   Siri to SysAdmin – "QA box is down due to recent patch, please revert it back to promote the build."

3. **Testing** – More testing of builds, automating running regression suites and figure out running most critical test cases driven by self-learning AI and Chatbot.

   Siri to Developer – "The most critical feature test cases "payment" has not run and it has not completed the test coverage. It's risk to build deployment."

4. **Incident Management** – Chatbot interacting with users, understanding their concerns and taking help from RPA bots to create incidents on different tools.

   SysAdmin to Siri – "our London CI Box is not responding, please raise a ticket and inform the respective team"

5. **Self-Healing** – AI powered DevOps that has inbuilt intelligence to proactively learn, notify common infrastructure issues and act to fix the issue automatically without any manual intervention.

   SysAdmin to Siri – "May you please get the logs of the box ip 10.10.192.168?"

6. **Log Retrieval** – Chatbot can help to analyze the root cause of the underlying issues by retrieving logs from the multiple machines that are running under multiple services.

   Siri to SysAdmin – "We've noticed IIS server was not responding. Based on our previous diagnosis and action, restarted the IIS Server. And, it's all ok now."

Many business owners are just beginning to understand what benefits "ChatOps" can bring to them. But at same time, hearing ChatOps sounds the death of DevOps or System Admin, but that is not the case. ChatOps simplifies operations life by automating routine monotonous activities, foster faster communication channel and empowering business stakeholders DIY (Do it yourself). But time is not very far away, when the bots will take over the charge in the software development processes.

Madan Upadhyay, CEO and Founder, Emergen Teck

Security

Security

Role of Security in DevOps

Data is the lifeblood of any organization. Today's organizations face a growing number of complex risks to their IT systems from external as well as internal sources. All this calls for ingraining security in every part of your DevOps lifecycle, ensuring compliance with your organization's security standards.

DevSecOps

DevOps security is all about securing the application, architecture, toolchains, pipelines and much more in an organization embracing DevOps. While it's clear that security should be embedded throughout the entire DevOps lifecycle, how do you make it a part of your organizational culture? Securing DevOps is not an easy task but when security becomes the default organizational culture for DevOps, it translates to what DevSecOps is all about.

Key Assessment Objectives

- Security assessment for DevOps enables identification of best practices to identify misconfigurations and provide guided remediation steps.
- It helps mitigate risk tied to data loss tied to misconfigurations.
- It enables risk management and security compliance of cloud-based, on-premises and hybrid systems.
- It enables automation of processes for assessment and authorization, remediation and ongoing compliance.

Key Practices Summary

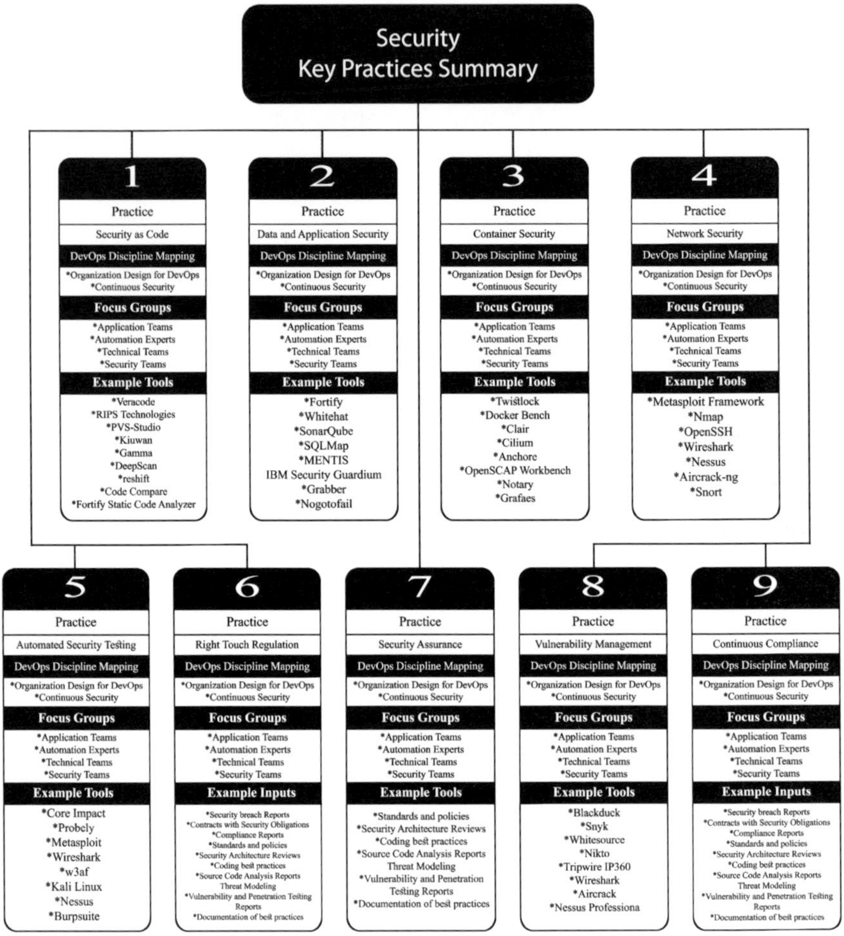

Security as Code

DevOps security encompasses protecting the entire DevOps environment from threats or risks through strategies, policies, workflows and technology. "Security as Code" refers to applying security policies in a codified manner to the DevOps pipeline at every phase.

Why Assess?

- Enables organizations to build software with a reduced attack surface that is both quick to deploy and restore
- Enables higher security and improved compliance with lower financial risk due to security breaches

Key Practice Summary

1
Practice
Security as Code
DevOps Discipline Mapping
*Organization Design for DevOps *Continuous Security
Focus Groups
*Application Teams *Automation Experts *Technical Teams *Security Teams
Example Tools
*Veracode *RIPS Technologies *PVS-Studio *Kiuwan *Gamma *DeepScan *reshift *Code Compare *Fortify Static Code Analyzer

Assessment Questions

**Questions to be scored on a scale of 1 to 5 (5 being ideal)*

***OSNA implies Objective Score Not Applicable*

Question	Score
1. To what extent is your Security strategy integrated with the principles of zero trust design?	(1) (2) (3) (4) (5)
2. To what extent have you adopted "**Security as code**"? In other words, to what extent have your security policies and requirements been codified as user stories? Look out for examples.	(1) (2) (3) (4) (5)
3. To what extent are your security officers acting as true advisors of building security as opposed to only gatekeepers of security checks?	(1) (2) (3) (4) (5)
4. To what extent does your security team own the collective responsibility of ensuring secure and breach free deployments? How do they make this happen?	(1) (2) (3) (4) (5)
5. To what extent are your runtime event monitoring and alert mechanisms effective?	(1) (2) (3) (4) (5)
6. To what extent are your runtime policy enforcement mechanisms effective?	(1) (2) (3) (4) (5)
7. To what extent do your security policies and mechanisms ensure protection of business-critical applications and sensitive data from Man In The Middle (MITM) attacks?	(1) (2) (3) (4) (5)
8. To what extent do you firewall, antivirus and certificate pinning policies and mechanisms ensure protection of business-critica applications and sensitive data from data and network security thefts and threats?	(1) (2) (3) (4) (5)
9. To what extent do you have an effective mechanism for continuous vulnerability management?	(1) (2) (3) (4) (5)
10. To what extent do your security measures enable workload isolation across public, private or hybrid cloud?	(1) (2) (3) (4) (5)
11. To what extent do your security measures enable API access control and identity management across public, private or hybrid cloud?	(1) (2) (3) (4) (5)
12. In the case of container-based architectures, to what extent do your security measures discover runtime vulnerabilities on the host such as privilege escalation, code injection and data exfiltration?	(1) (2) (3) (4) (5)
13. To what extent do you have active Special Interest Groups (SIGs) for security that are champions for reinforcing the security culture within the organization?	(1) (2) (3) (4) (5)
14. What are the different security practices in your organization or team that ingrain the security and compliance posture and at the same time, do not compromise with the delivery velocity?	**OSNA
15. To what extent do your development teams practice Test Driven Security? Look out for examples	(1) (2) (3) (4) (5)

16.	To what extent do you have automated mechanisms for penetration testing in place?	1 2 3 4 5
17.	To what extent are security testing tools integrated into the build pipeline and are run by developers on every commit?	1 2 3 4 5
18.	To what extent do you have consumable dashboard analytics that can plainly demonstrate how healthy an application is in terms of security?	1 2 3 4 5
19.	To what extent are secure coding principles integrated into your software development lifecycle (SDLC) components?	1 2 3 4 5
20.	What are the different vulnerability scoring algorithms available?	**OSNA
21.	To what extent do you identify and prioritize risks using advanced vulnerability scoring algorithms?	1 2 3 4 5
22.	To what extent do you provide tailored advice, incident assistance and audit support to teams as a part of managing vulnerabilities?	1 2 3 4 5
23.	To what extent do you have a comprehensive discovery and profiling mechanism in place for all network assets?	1 2 3 4 5

Leaders Think

Security as Code is using DevOps automation practices to enhance your application security practices by automating the collection of data and shifting security testing left into the daily workflow of the team.

Thomas Stiehm, CTO, Coveros, Inc.

Security as code is a process and policy driven approach where you start with assessing the asset inventory and embed security in the enterprise product lifecycle management (PLM) and technology lifecycle management (TLM) processes. From the time, an asset – be it physical or virtual gets acquired till the time it gets decommissioned, security has to be a critical part of the workflow including the business as usual (BAU) management processes like patching and so on. Security should be codified for data and applications, containers, networks and all infrastructure in any organization and automating or making such processes rule-based enables higher efficiency and reduced financial and business risk.

Manish Nashine, Director, Dun and Bradstreet

Data and Application Security

Security and compliance are critical aspects of product delivery. Business Data is the intellectual asset and lifeblood and competitive differentiator of any organization, which makes security an absolute imperative. Application security is a practice of adding security features or functionality to software to prevent it from multiple risks and threats, e.g. denial of service attacks, data breaches or theft and so on.

Why Assess?

There is a phenomenal amount of data traversing the network through cloud environments at any given point in time. This makes it imperative to control and protect the transfer of sensitive or personal information not only at rest but also in flight.

When risk assessment, security testing and compliance evaluation aren't built into the applications, CI/CD pipeline, releases fail and cause delays, security vulnerabilities threaten Production and IT governance violations result in expensive penalties, financial losses and tarnished reputation, all of which can't be afforded by organizations.

Key Practice Summary

2
Practice
Data and Application Security
DevOps Discipline Mapping
*Organization Design for DevOps *Continuous Security
Focus Groups
*Application Teams *Automation Experts *Technical Teams *Security Teams
Example Tools
*Fortify *Whitehat *SonarQube *SQLMap *MENTIS IBM Security Guardium *Grabber *Nogotofail

Assessment Questions

**Questions to be scored on a scale of 1 to 5 (5 being ideal)*

***OSNA implies Objective Score Not Applicable*

Question		Score
1.	To what extent is security integrated as a part of your overall DevOps strategy?	① ② ③ ④ ⑤
2.	How do you shift security and compliance concerns left, so they can be addressed in Development?	**OSNA
3.	To what extent are there measures applied to uncover security vulnerabilities in the application?	① ② ③ ④ ⑤
4.	How do you visualize and evaluate security vulnerabilities and IT governance violations?	**OSNA
5.	What are the current mechanisms in place that allow you to capture the critical release chain of custody needed for software security?	**OSNA
6.	To what extent do you carry out Static Application Security Testing (SAST) towards application security?	① ② ③ ④ ⑤
7.	How do you integrate automated security and compliance testing into the software delivery pipeline?	**OSNA
8.	To what extent do you have checkpoints in your CI-CD pipeline/ workflow at which application security tools run? What are those checkpoints?	① ② ③ ④ ⑤
9.	To what extent do you have a vulnerability assessment process integrated into your build chain?	① ② ③ ④ ⑤
10.	To what extent do your security analyzers take care of security and compliance with regulatory standards demanded by the domain, customer or end user?	① ② ③ ④ ⑤
11.	For solutions or workloads that you have moved to the cloud, to what extent do you assess the infrastructure, application and data security risks that could potentially disrupt your business or compromise your security? What are your existing mechanisms for the same?	① ② ③ ④ ⑤
12.	To what extent do policies and checkpoints ensure the security for containerized applications deployed in the cloud?	① ② ③ ④ ⑤
13.	To what extent do your infrastructure definitions include security checks that are automatically executed as part of your security and infrastructure management policies?	① ② ③ ④ ⑤
14.	To what extent does your system include dynamic scans of the code as part of an early round of automated testing?	① ② ③ ④ ⑤
15.	For every increment of the code that is added, to what extent are these scans intelligent enough to detect any potential errors or threats?	① ② ③ ④ ⑤
16.	To what extent are there checks in place that can flag unreachable code that can pose security threats?	① ② ③ ④ ⑤

17.	To what extent is the code that is continuously integrated also continuously scanned for such security aspects?	1 2 3 4 5
18.	To what extent are Security specialists invited to project kickoffs that involve DevOps?	1 2 3 4 5
19.	To what extent do you run Static Application Security Testing (SAST) scans on your nightly builds?	1 2 3 4 5
20.	To what extent do you execute Runtime Application Self Protection (RASP)?	1 2 3 4 5
21.	To what extent do you run interactive application security testing (IAST) to force failures to improve vulnerability patterns?	1 2 3 4 5
22.	To what extent do you ensure that the changes in code committed during that day are secure and free of threats?	1 2 3 4 5
23.	To what extent are there any mechanisms/plans for dynamic application security testing (DAST) into your SDLC?	1 2 3 4 5
24.	In case DAST is embedded in your SDLC already, what are the kind of vulnerabilities that have been detected so far? How have they been addressed?	**OSNA
25.	To what extent are developers trained on the techniques to secure coding? Look out for specific examples	1 2 3 4 5
26.	To what extent is the code quality assessed for potential security threats?	1 2 3 4 5
27.	To what extent are there encryption mechanisms in place to ensure data security for data at rest and in transit?	1 2 3 4 5
28.	To what extent are there encryption mechanisms in place towards hardware security?	1 2 3 4 5

Leaders Think

Data and Application Security start with a secure application development lifecycle. There are multiple tools that may be used for purpose of static application scanning, dynamic application testing, manual pen testing, dynamic pen testing that not only allow you to lock down code changes with an objective to assess threats but also help you evaluate encryption options, access rights and audit permissions. Web application and mobile application firewalls may be implemented with signature-based approaches to detect vulnerabilities like cross-site scripting and so on. All of these are crucial to securing data and application security in today's digital world.

Manish Nashine, Director, Dun and Bradstreet

Container Security

Container security refers to protecting the integrity of containers. That means anything and everything held within a container, applications to infrastructure. It includes securing the images, the containers that hold those images and thc hosts that are running the containers. In general, continuous container security for the enterprise is about securing the application and the container pipeline.

Why Assess?

- Running containers on a distributed system in today's growing hybrid cloud adoptions makes container security a critical factor to consider both for business and end customers
- Containers run on shared hosts and leverage multiple components to deliver an entire solution which makes container security all the more important
- Container security is key to achieving speed and efficiency along with no data breaches or financial risks

Key Practice Summary

3
Practice
Container Security
DevOps Discipline Mapping
*Organization Design for DevOps *Continuous Security
Focus Groups
*Application Teams *Automation Experts *Technical Teams *Security Teams
Example Tools
*Twistlock *Docker Bench *Clair *Cilium *Anchore *OpenSCAP Workbench *Notary *Grafaes

Assessment Questions

**Questions to be scored on a scale of 1 to 5 (5 being ideal)*

***OSNA implies Objective Score Not Applicable*

****SDN (S/W Defined Working)*

Question	Score
1. What percentage of your cybersecurity incidents over the last 4 quarters involve container-related security issues?	**OSNA
2. To what extent do your current security mechanisms ensure containers cannot be proliferated in the way they are configured or deployed?	1 2 3 4 5
3. What is the time to detect a compromised container in your network?	**OSNA
4. What are the cybersecurity tools and controls being leveraged to manage containers?	**OSNA
5. To what extent do you ensure that containers are always deployed with a hardened configuration?	1 2 3 4 5
6. To what extent do your current security mechanisms ensure that every container is signed and authenticated and has content that can be trusted?	1 2 3 4 5
7. To what extent do your current security mechanisms ensure secrets management of passwords and keys by making sure that they are never embedded in the images or need a part of the deployment process to ensure full content trust?	1 2 3 4 5
8. To what extent do your current security policies and practices ensure host security for containers?	1 2 3 4 5
9. To what extent are you aware of your cloud provider's security policies for ensuring your data from other cloud tenants?	1 2 3 4 5
10. To what extent are your cloud provider's security mechanisms automated?	1 2 3 4 5
11. To what extent do you audit your virtual environment to ensure that your cloud provider is compliant to your organization's security norms and policies?	1 2 3 4 5
12. To what extent do you map every Customer's security policy model to his/her OpenStack and contrail network policy framework and security group constructs?	1 2 3 4 5
13. To what extent does your security policy define the types of workload/instance traffic that are allowed and denied for access by OpenStack security groups?	1 2 3 4 5
14. To what extent do your hypervisor deployments avoid security risks?	1 2 3 4 5
15. To what extent are there encryption mechanisms in place towards hardware security?	1 2 3 4 5

Leaders Think

Container security includes everything that is needed to protect integrity of information in the container. Security the container pipeline, the deployment environment and infrastructure, the container data is of critical importance hcre. Containers also need to be securely integrated with the enterprise security tools and adhere to or enhance the existing enterprise security policies and processes. Static security checklists need to scale up to meet the enterprise needs for container security with a firm focus on runtime checks and governance.

Manish Nashine, Director, Dun and Bradstreet

Network Security

Network security is a discipline of ensuring security of the network with surveillance on operations that prevent and monitor unauthorized access, data theft over the network, misuse, modification or denial of network accessible resources.

Why Assess?

- Network security is becoming increasingly important in recent times due to the growing number of hackers stealing sensitive data over not so secure networks resulting in huge financial, security and reputational risks
- Network security is vital to prevent industry sabotage and espionage. Other security concerns also revolve around user traffic
- Network safety for DevOps transformation addresses the goals of safety and speed both in complete alignment for all applications in scope

Key Practice Summary

4
Practice
Network Security
DevOps Discipline Mapping
*Organization Design for DevOps *Continuous Security
Focus Groups
*Application Teams *Automation Experts *Technical Teams *Security Teams
Example Tools
*Metasploit Framework *Nmap *OpenSSH *Wireshark *Nessus *Aircrack-ng *Snort

Assessment Questions

**Questions to be scored on a scale of 1 to 5 (5 being ideal)*

***OSNA implies Objective Score Not Applicable*

Question		Score
1.	How often does your network security review happen during the development process?	**OSNA
2.	To what extent is your fiber optic layer secured through cryptographic algorithms that prevent hacking for data inflight?	① ② ③ ④ ⑤
3.	To what extent is your development team aware that the code it has written will not violate the security policies?	① ② ③ ④ ⑤
4.	To what extent does the security team review license conditions with legal for all new software and open source platforms being leveraged?	① ② ③ ④ ⑤
5.	To what extent does the security team enforce and ensure segregation of duties and limited access to production environments?	① ② ③ ④ ⑤
6.	To what extent is automated and secure patch management implemented for applications and networks?	① ② ③ ④ ⑤
7.	To what extent is automated and secure patch management implemented for open source components?	① ② ③ ④ ⑤

Leaders Think

Network security is that part of infrastructure security that deals with securing enterprise networks and data from being manipulated, misused or compromised. This includes multiple areas such as virus and malware detection, file and email security, data loss protection, behavioural analytics, firewalls, network segmentation, endpoint security, security information and event management, web and wireless security and network access control and so on. All with an end objective to achieve a more secure enterprise network not vulnerable to web attacks and social engineering.

Manish Nashine, Director, Dun and Bradstreet

Automated Security Testing

Automated unit, integration and acceptance tests are important quality controls in executing a CI-CD pipeline. Most often, security tests are omitted from the overall testing workflow because of the myth and wrong belief that security testing is solely the responsibility of the security team.

Why Assess?

- To ensure the objectives of security testing and automate the tests with a specified success and acceptance criteria
- Enables security scanning of the application and infrastructure along with security testing application logic

Key Practice Summary

5
Practice
Automated Security Testing
DevOps Discipline Mapping
*Organization Design for DevOps *Continuous Security
Focus Groups
*Application Teams *Automation Experts *Technical Teams *Security Teams
Example Tools
*Core Impact *Probely *Metasploit *Wireshark *w3af *Kali Linux *Nessus *Burpsuite

Assessment Questions

**Questions to be scored on a scale of 1 to 5 (5 being ideal)*

***OSNA implies Objective Score Not Applicable*

Question		Score
1.	To what extent is your DevOps approach with security testing objectives?	(1) (2) (3) (4) (5)
2.	To what extent are automated security tests executed in parallel to the build with appropriate review and governance from security experts?	(1) (2) (3) (4) (5)
3.	To what extent does automated security testing ensure that the security team is notified of and can manually stop delivery if test failures indicate the presence of an unacceptable risk?	(1) (2) (3) (4) (5)
4.	To what extent do your automated security tests ensure application readiness for any possible outbreak or mass attack?	(1) (2) (3) (4) (5)
5.	To what extent have you implemented automated security testing frameworks to test application readiness to any such liability attack?	(1) (2) (3) (4) (5)
6.	To what extent are your automated security testing mechanisms effective in discovering security and other defects not found in earlier rounds of testing?	(1) (2) (3) (4) (5)
7.	To what extent are there encryption mechanisms in place towards hardware security?	(1) (2) (3) (4) (5)

Leaders Think

Most organizations use orchestration platforms for vulnerabilities management that provide self-sufficient and built in checks for development teams leveraging these platforms to deploy their code or upgrade versions and perform the security checks with each such event to ensure vulnerabilities are identified and mitigated. Automated Security Testing ensures that any violations when teams do not perform checks or ignore risks in the code are identified and addressed by respective functions or groups.

Manish Nashine, Director, Dun and Bradstreet

Right Touch Regulation

Right-touch regulation is a practice that ensures the level of regulation is in line with the risk and regulatory requirements of the product, customer and governed by contractual compliances and regulatory norms for the geography where the product or services will be deployed or consumed. This is a very pragmatic approach for regulatory mandates in multiple industries such as banking and financial services, healthcare and so on.

Why Assess?

- Right touch regulation is needed to be compliant to regulations as per industry, geography and domain norms and hence assessment is important.
- Enables taking security-related decisions when considering open source software as well as third-party products for system integration.

Key Practice Summary

6
Practice
Right Touch Regulation
DevOps Discipline Mapping
*Organization Design for DevOps *Continuous Security
Focus Groups
*Application Teams *Automation Experts *Technical Teams *Security Teams
Example Inputs
*Security breach Reports *Contracts with Security Obligations *Compliance Reports *Standards and policies *Security Architecture Reviews *Coding best practices *Source Code Analysis Reports Threat Modeling *Vulnerability and Penetration Testing Reports *Documentation of best practices

Assessment Questions

**Questions to be scored on a scale of 1 to 5 (5 being ideal)*

***OSNA implies Objective Score Not Applicable*

Question		Score
1.	To what extent do you design principles and approaches foster **right-touch regulation**?	1 2 3 4 5
2.	To what extent is compliance, audit and risk integrated with the overall DevOps Strategy for the organization?	1 2 3 4 5
3.	To what extent are compliance requirements and policies codified and have an audit trail? Look for examples.	1 2 3 4 5
4.	To what extent are your test environments automatically provisioned?	1 2 3 4 5
5.	To what extent do you extend the developer mindset into the compliance, audit and risk function?	1 2 3 4 5
6.	To what extent is compliance governance and reporting simplified as a process in the context of the overall organization? Look for examples.	1 2 3 4 5
7.	To what extent are regulations like General Data Protection Regulation (GDPR) integrated with your DevOps strategy? Look out for the complete workflow across the organization.	1 2 3 4 5
8.	To what extent is separation of duties integrated with your DevOps Strategy?	1 2 3 4 5
9.	To what extent are your third-party compliance software and COTS products compliant with regulatory requirements?	1 2 3 4 5

Leaders Think

Right-touch regulation means understanding the problem before jumping to the solution. It makes sure that the level of regulation is proportionate to the level of risk. Too much regulation of your development practices may not be essential when the risk involved is not as huge. Plus DevOps practices such as easy code reversal are there for the back-up. Regulatory compliance is mandatory in regulated industries like Healthcare, Banking and Finance. By adopting the DevOps automation techniques organizational assets can be better controlled, audited and protected. Start with understanding and defining the problem, quantify and qualify the risks, use regulation only when necessary, check for unintended consequences and always be ready to respond to change in the DevOps world.

Sanjeev Kulkarni, CEO and Founder, Productshaala

Security Assurance

Software Security Assurance (SSA) is a key practice of ensuring that software is designed to operate at a security level that will prevent any harm resulting from the alteration, manipulation, loss, inaccuracy, misuse or unavailability of the data and resources that it uses, controls and protects.

Why Assess?

- It enables visibility into the security posture for all systems and devices in a heterogeneous enterprise
- It enables an organization to define and optimize its defense mechanisms by making sure that security systems are configured properly and performing as expected
- It ensures compliance with security mandates, company policies and industry regulations
- It aligns IT operations, security operations and business operations to increase organizational efficiency and effectiveness

Key Practice Summary

7
Practice
Security Assurance
DevOps Discipline Mapping
*Organization Design for DevOps *Continuous Security
Focus Groups
*Application Teams *Automation Experts *Technical Teams *Security Teams
Example Tools
*Standards and policies *Security Architecture Reviews *Coding best practices *Source Code Analysis Reports Threat Modeling *Vulnerability and Penetration Testing Reports *Documentation of best practices

Assessment Questions

**Questions to be scored on a scale of 1 to 5 (5 being ideal)*

***OSNA implies Objective Score Not Applicable*

Question		Score
1.	To what extent is Security Assurance an integral part of your DevOps/ DevSecOps and Security Strategy?	① ② ③ ④ ⑤
2.	To what extent is there a process defined and implemented for a formal security audit/review to happen at every phase/iteration of the software lifecycle for potentially shippable product increments developed?	① ② ③ ④ ⑤
3.	To what extent are there security checks for any middleware in the programs within the scope of review?	① ② ③ ④ ⑤
4.	To what extent are there security checkpoints for any architectural-specific vulnerabilities and the data flow through the code?	① ② ③ ④ ⑤
5.	To what extent are there audits or checks for software security risks as part of the overall delivery risk management process?	① ② ③ ④ ⑤
6.	To what extent is the data security validated when passed from application servers to databases?	① ② ③ ④ ⑤
7.	To what extent does the application software store any nonsensitive information that can be used to probe secrets?	① ② ③ ④ ⑤
8.	To what extent is the software reviewed for complexity and alternatives explored to reduce the complexity?	① ② ③ ④ ⑤
9.	To what extent are there tools established to be used for various stages of the life cycle for assessing security?	① ② ③ ④ ⑤
10.	To what extent is security testing performed as part of unit and system integration?	① ② ③ ④ ⑤
11.	To what extent does the team define any product-specific or service-specific security requirements as part of its development cycle?	① ② ③ ④ ⑤
12.	To what extent does the team conduct an architectural risk analysis or threat modeling as part of its product lifecycle and define appropriate mitigations?	① ② ③ ④ ⑤
13.	To what extent does the team perform static code reviews in an automated manner to identify security defects introduced during coding?	① ② ③ ④ ⑤
14.	To what extent does the team perform automated dynamic security testing to identify common security vulnerabilities?	① ② ③ ④ ⑤
15.	To what extent does the team triage security defects identified from the above activities and remediate them as part of its lifecycle?	① ② ③ ④ ⑤
16.	To what extent does the team have a supply chain risk management process to manage the security and integrity of sourced components?	① ② ③ ④ ⑤

17.	To what extent does the team conduct proper roadmap planning to identify future steps for remediating any unmitigated findings?	(1) (2) (3) (4) (5)
18.	To what extent do the appropriate levels of management in the organization review and sign off on the security posture of the product?	(1) (2) (3) (4) (5)

Leaders Think

Most organizations that are now embarking on a journey towards DevOps have realized that security should be ingrained in the organization DNA and cannot be a separate layer in isolation. Security Assurance includes implementation of security checks and attributes throughout the product and technology life cycle. It includes secure architecture and design analysis with special focus on analysis of business logic, data, constraints, interfaces through control mechanisms like inspections, code reviews and design reviews. Thus said, it focusses on program level and application level security along with security for all technology workflows within the enterprise stack.

Manish Nashine, Director, Dun and Bradstreet

Vulnerability Management

Vulnerability management is a key practice that enables vulnerabilities in software and services to be identified, classified, prioritized and evaluate their risks and impacts. It involves vulnerability scanning and also risk acceptance, rcmediation and so on.

Why Assess?

- Helps to identify, classify and quantify the vulnerabilities in the software product to be released and in the surrounding environment
- Equips organizations to formulate appropriate response mechanisms to address these vulnerabilities from a risk and security perspective

Key Practice Summary

8
Practice
Vulnerability Management
DevOps Discipline Mapping
*Organization Design for DevOps *Continuous Security
Focus Groups
*Application Teams *Automation Experts *Technical Teams *Security Teams
Example Tools
*Blackduck *Snyk *Whitesource *Nikto *Tripwire IP360 *Wireshark *Aircrack *Nessus Professional

Assessment Questions

**Questions to be scored on a scale of 1 to 5 (5 being ideal)*

***OSNA implies Objective Score Not Applicable*

	Question	Score
1.	To what extent is the vulnerability remediation process defined, implemented and integrated with your DevOps strategy?	① ② ③ ④ ⑤
2.	To what extent is there a process defined and implemented to report all vulnerabilities in the released software?	① ② ③ ④ ⑤
3.	To what extent is there a process defined and implemented to issue security advisories or alerts to business and customers to notify remediation of security vulnerabilities?	① ② ③ ④ ⑤
4.	To what extent does the organization-level policy require its secure development process for all applications and patch releases?	① ② ③ ④ ⑤
5.	To what extent do the team's verification activity results drive changes in the implementation of secure architecture and coding standards?	① ② ③ ④ ⑤
6.	To what extent are the development and testing teams audited for compliance with security policy routinely (e.g., per release, yearly)?	① ② ③ ④ ⑤
7.	How are vulnerabilities in any third party open source libraries used identified, assessed for risk and mitigated?	**OSNA
8.	To what extent are all critical applications tested and assessed for business logic and security runtime and randomly?	① ② ③ ④ ⑤

Leaders Think

Vulnerability Management has been gaining pronounced attention in recent times. The main objective of this practice is to identify security holes in your assets, report, prioritize, remediate and verify that the risks have been eliminated. Asset discovery using mapping scans or light inventory scans helps you understand what to scan on your network. Static and dynamic asset tags together help you categorize assets as business critical or otherwise. Scheduled authenticated scanning helps you receive best results leveraging the power of automation. Customized reports eg. patch reports can be generated based on stakeholder requirements which feeds as an input to the remediation phase. Prioritized remediation activities also include validation mechanisms eg. segregation of duties to ensure resolution of vulnerabilities identified and reported.

Manish Nashine, Director, Dun and Bradstreet

Continuous Compliance

Compliance, being critical to most organizations, is imperative to incorporate into their larger DevOps culture. Continuous compliance is all about delivering compliant products and services that can not only cut your operational costs, improve efficiencies, improve customer satisfaction but also reduce risks from multiple business perspectives.

Why Assess?

- Enables maintaining continuous security
- Enables a common framework of compliance irrespective of technology stack and architectural landscape

Key Practice Summary

9

Practice

Continuous Compliance

DevOps Discipline Mapping

*Organization Design for DevOps
*Continuous Security

Focus Groups

*Application Teams
*Automation Experts
*Technical Teams
*Security Teams

Example Inputs

*Security breach Reports
*Contracts with Security Obligations
*Compliance Reports
*Standards and policies
*Security Architecture Reviews
*Coding best practices
*Source Code Analysis Reports
Threat Modeling
*Vulnerability and Penetration Testing Reports
*Documentation of best practices

Assessment Questions

**Questions to be scored on a scale of 1 to 5 (5 being ideal)*

***OSNA implies Objective Score Not Applicable*

Question		Score
1.	To what extent do you have a clarity of all changes in every project that are at different stages with a clear view of all functional and non-functional compliance levels?	① ② ③ ④ ⑤
2.	To what extent do your teams practice continuous integration and have audit trails of all of the software development activities in a release?	① ② ③ ④ ⑤
3.	To what extent are your builds tagged appropriately to ensure that the deployments are reviewed and monitored to stop unauthorized changes moving forward?	① ② ③ ④ ⑤
4.	Are all infrastructure provisioning scripts under configuration control?	**OSNA
5.	To what extent are infrastructure provisioning scripts verifiable and testable which can be consistent, reliable and reproduce results with no change in configurations?	① ② ③ ④ ⑤

Leaders Think

Compliance must never be an afterthought in Software Development. As in any civilized set up we are required to follow certain rules and regulations - and that applies to our software development practices as well. Regulatory compliance may be tedious and cumbersome at times but is an essential pill. If you think the price you must pay for rapid development and integration is to sideline compliance responsibilities - you are doing it wrong! The company may get short term gains by cutting compliance corners, but there will be huge costs involved in case of a regulatory audit. And think about the attorney fees, penalties and loss of reputation.

Sanjeev Kulkarni, CEO and Founder, Productshaala

Part 3

Assessment Outcomes

Assessment Outcomes

Typically, when organizations want to do a DevOps Assessment, they have certain strategic priorities in their minds which they seek to address through DevOps. Transformation is a journey, not an overnight change and hence it is implicit that any such initiative is a multi-year program that needs a sustained focus and continued momentum.

Assessments are typically budgeted based on the priority areas in the scope and size of the portfolios and representative programs being assessed.

Assessment Scoring and Analysis

We spoke about the key areas that fall in the purview of a typical DevOps Assessment. These different areas may be of different priorities to business During the assessment kickoff, the relative ranking and priorities of these areas are frozen post discussion with the different stakeholders. This decides the weightages and importance of these areas in the overall DevOps Assessment scores.

For example, the focus area – Leadership and Commitment has 5 key practices for assessment as below

1. Leadership Agility
2. Strategy, Vision and Goals
3. Change Ambassadors Agility
4. DevOps Team Topology
5. Innovation

The default weightage of each area is 20%; however, if Leadership Agility is of prime importance to the stakeholders, they can choose to assign it as 35% as the case may be. The rest of the areas will get redistributed for priority weightages. Different areas will be ranked and analyzed based on interviews, observations, interaction with application teams, enabling functions and support groups and assessment of project, program and portfolio workflows and value streams.

Key Deliverables from an Assessment

Key deliverables from the DevOps Assessment are listed in the below table

Deliverable	Scope of Coverage
Assessment Recommendations Report with Scorecard	• Score of each key practice area • Gaps, observations and recommendations in each area • Capability upgrade recommendations for the portfolio (Training Plan, including people and skills identification based on the gap analysis done and budgeting for DevOps Transformation) • Recommended DevOps practices and tools • Recommended DevOps metrics • Proposed tools and CI CD Pipeline for pilot projects
Prioritization Matrix for Assessment Action Items	• Action items from Assessment Recommendations prioritized collaboratively with stakeholders considering implementation ease, duration, technical feasibility and rated in order of importance
DevOps Progression Model	• Measure of where your organization stands on the DevOps continuum
DevOps Transformation Roadmap	• Prioritization Matrix outcomes on a timescale to identify near, mid and long-term objectives
Gap Analysis Report	• Current State Analysis and Target State View with DevOps adopted

**Prioritization Matrix, DevOps Progression Model and DevOps Transformation Roadmap are discussed in the next chapter*

What to expect in a Recommendations Report?

A recommendations report is typically an outcome of focus group discussions of stakeholders, project, program and team assessments for risks, current competency and maturity on various practices and behaviours, engineering practices adopted and so on.

Typically, the objective of a recommendations report is to highlight the gaps observed during assessment, deviations from practices that would reflect the DevOps ways of working and areas of conflict or risk from future delivery and product quality perspective.

For each focus area assessed, the recommendations report will clearly articulate the observations, gaps and subsequent collaborative discussions with teams and stakeholders will enable facilitating the plan to close this gap. The action items from these conversations get listed as product backlog items on the overall transformation backlog.

A recommendations report is a vital input to create a DevOps transformation roadmap which includes people transformation, program transformation, technical acceleration, leadership grooming for DevOps and a learning plan for skills enablement.

Most executives report that this report revitalizes their DevOps transformation journey by giving them a right pragmatic start with a holistic organization view and key focus areas to concentrate their energies and investments on.

What NOT to expect in a Recommendations Report?

- ROI from DevOps Transformation
- A finish date to mark your organization as "DevOps Compliant"
- % of new customers acquired as a result of implementing DevOps
- % of increase in your revenues and wallet share after implementing DevOps

DevOps Assessment Report

A DevOps Assessment Report (including a detailed Assessment Scorecard and recommendations) is an outcome of this entire assessment exercise. It enlists detailed observations on various focus areas and alongside shares recommendations for deliberation for the enterprise. This report is a powerful weapon in terms of creating a transformation roadmap and a change management plan to achieve successful transformation with DevOps.

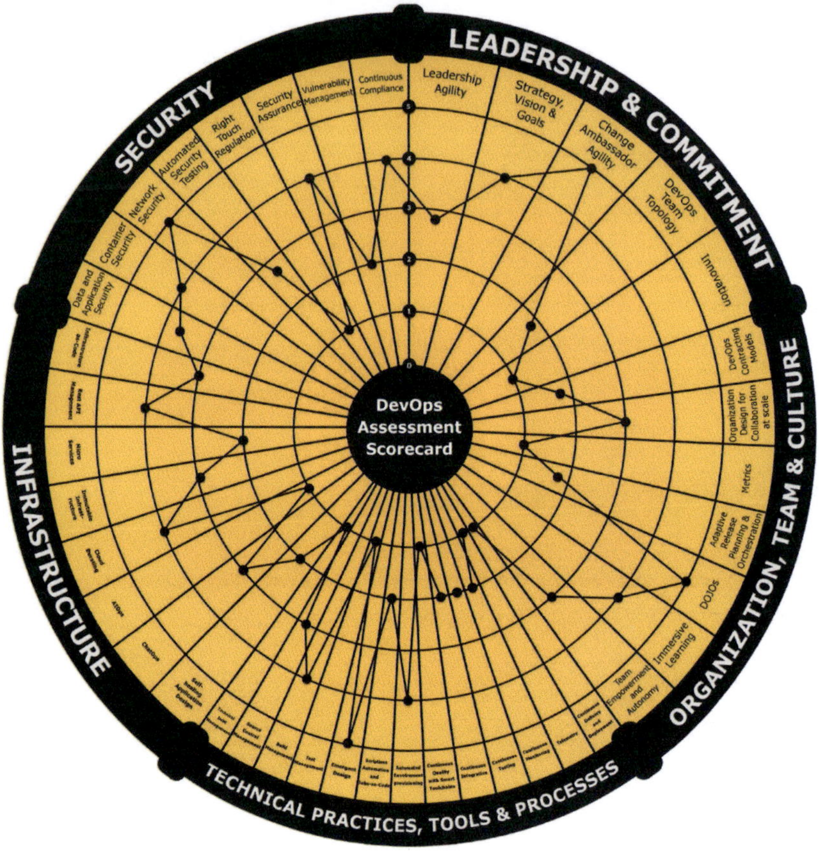

DevOps Assessment Scorecard

Focus Area	Action Item / Recommendation
Leadership	Some of the status reports from teams implementing DevOps are green-phased by the time they reach senior management and issues or risks that need explicit attention or support do not appear explicitly. Senior management should be more engaged with teams through floor connects, formal and informal reviews that will build more visibility into progress and break the ice to ask for support where needed
Leadership	A designated transformation owner must be identified to ensure transformation action items for leadership are progressing and adapting course where needed
Leadership	Leaders must budget out time and budget for innovation each quarter. The current innovation strategy does not effectively demonstrate how the outcomes of innovation activities in previous quarters were leveraged to business benefits
Leadership	Leaders must budget out time and budget for thought leadership in technical and business practices each quarter and engage people to participate and contribute in such forums
Organizational Culture	DevOps teams cannot operate in isolation. Application teams need to embrace DevOps practices in order to drive DevOps
Organizational Culture	A DevOps CoE can facilitate DevOps through training, improved awareness or connecting people with existing DevOps projects. Executing the project or program in DevOps must be the KRA of application development and maintenance teams and not that of the CoE
Organizational Culture	Retrospectives carried out at the end of each iteration need to be checked for conversion into findings that are actionable and what has been done on actions from previous retrospectives
Technical Practices	Acceptance tests performed for deployment tooling to be integrated with security tests
Technical Practices	Automated feedback loops to be implemented between tests that spot errors along with correction code with appropriate notifications and triggers. The current build process is largely manual
Technical Practices	Current testing tools do not provide an integrated unit performance, security testing services or end-to-end automation. This area needs to be worked on to ensure continuous integration and delivery
Technical Practices	Eliminate database coupling using microservices architecture for application X and application Y
Technical Practices	DBA reviews for deploying database change scripts are conducted much later in the cycle and very near to the release, which makes it an expensive cost to change. Explore version-or-source controlling the database (with rollbacks and audit trail) as an option
Technical Practices	Automated build process on code check-in is missing or inconsistent for most applications. This needs to be implemented along with source control
Technical Practices	Databases are not being monitored for deadlocks or blocking processes, resulting in significant downtime in case of an outage. A proactive mechanism to address this needs to be created collaboratively and implemented
Technical Practices	Automate non-functional testing. The current process is largely manual

Technical Practices	Build in tracing and information in the pipeline and auto generation of release notes
Technical Practices	Maximize UAT automation
Technical Practices	Build process needs to be fully automated. No self service and scheduled full builds. Build artifacts are not maintained in repository and there are no build notifications for multiple applications
Infrastructure	No auto deployment scripts. No auto environment provisioning scripts for most applications. This process needs to be zero-touch
Infrastructure	Documentation duplication to be minimized within and across teams. Only create and provide documentation within the team that provides direct value. Merge similar documents to eliminate redundancy (where possible)
Infrastructure	Infrastructure Automation to be implemented. Currently, most of the configurations are largely manual
Security	Security Testing objectives to be aligned to DevOps approach
Security	Create automated security tests executed in parallel to the build with governance and review by the security experts
Security	Security team to be notified of test failures indicating presence of unacceptable risk. They should be empowered to manually block delivery in such cases
Security	Create automated security tests that ensure application readiness for any possible outbreak or mass attack
Security	Implement automated security testing frameworks to test application readiness to any such liability attack
Security	Vulnerabilities and leaks detected on new code through static code analysis need to be prioritized and fixed collaboratively
Security	Include automated security penetration testing as a standard part of the build and deployment workflow

Transformation Roadmap and ROI

DevOps Transformation Roadmap

A DevOps transformation roadmap is a high-level plan that acts as a vehicle to communicate the DevOps vision of the organization and the direction and steps an organization chooses to take towards their DevOps transformation. This is different from the DevOps transformation operating model or project plan which is much more detailed and should include a DevOps Assessment and a transformation roadmap as a listed milestone. The next set of DevOps transformation project plans may be created depending on specific business context, e.g. whether or not the organization is scaling their transformation.

Why Prepare a Transformation Roadmap for DevOps?

Many organizations that implement DevOps fail not because of increasing complexity of their technology landscapes but because of no clear direction. A roadmap helps address this gap and much more. Broadly, a roadmap helps address the following purposes.

- It provides a frame of prioritized action items and solutions that enables teams to gravitate independently towards the organizational goals of transformation.
- It provides clarity on how DevOps ways of working and these solutions will be key to influencing business outcomes.
- It helps to reduce resistance and serves as a strong foundation and helps in scaling the transformation rigor across the organization.

How to Create a Transformation Roadmap?

Creating the DevOps transformation roadmap is an arduous effort. While you may reference roadmaps of few other organizations, it important to recognize that every organization presents a unique proposition in terms of its own culture, challenges, roadblocks and readiness for DevOps, all of which must be factored when creating a DevOps transformation roadmap.

It is suggested that a DevOps assessor be present to collaborate and support in the roadmap creation using various techniques to facilitate navigating the discussions and facilitate in ensuring that the most appropriate milestones are included.

To arrive at this, the recommendations and observations from the DevOps Assessment. Report are discussed collaboratively with leadership and relevant stakeholders from each focus area and representative programs.

The outcomes from this discussion are converted into solutions to be picked up for implementation. A prioritization matrix is created based on the following parameters

- Business Value
    - Alignment to organizational/strategic objectives
    - Alignment to project/program/portfolio objectives
    - Estimated and quantified potential savings to project/program/portfolio
    - Estimated development and implementation effort
    - Ease of implementation
- Risk reduction / Opportunity enablement
- Time (calendar duration) to implement

A sample prioritization matrix is shown here for reference.

Prioritization Matrix for DevOps Assessment Recommendations and Action Items								
Solution	**Business Value (a)**	**Timing Impact (b)**	**Risk Reduction/ Opportunity Enablement (c)**	**Cost of Delay CoD = a + b + c**	**Duration in months (d)**	**WSJF Score = CoD/d**	**Execution Window**	**WSJF Ranking/ Priortization**
Range	1-10	1-10	1-10		1-24			
Establish a center of excellence for DevOps	5	6	6	17	3	6	Near Term	3
Focussed hiring for coaches	5	8	7	20	3	7	Near Term	2
Develop strategy for Chatops	9	5	5	19	10	2	Long Term	6
Establish a transformation program office and program owner	7	7	7	21	3	7	Near Term	2
Integrate security with acceptance tests	8	8	8	24	8	3	Mid Term	5
Maximize UAT Automation	8	8	10	26	7	4	Mid Term	4
Automate build process completely	10	5	10	25	3	8	Near Term	1

Solutions from the prioritization matrix get prioritized based on the WSJF ranking as per above parameters as agreed upon by the stakeholders. This in turn creates the Transformation Backlog.

Items from the Transformation Backlog are further groomed to be identified for picking up as low-hanging fruits/quick wins or for implementation over short, medium or longer term based on time to implement and other parameters. This generates a DevOps Transformation Roadmap.

A sample DevOps Roadmap is shown here for reference.

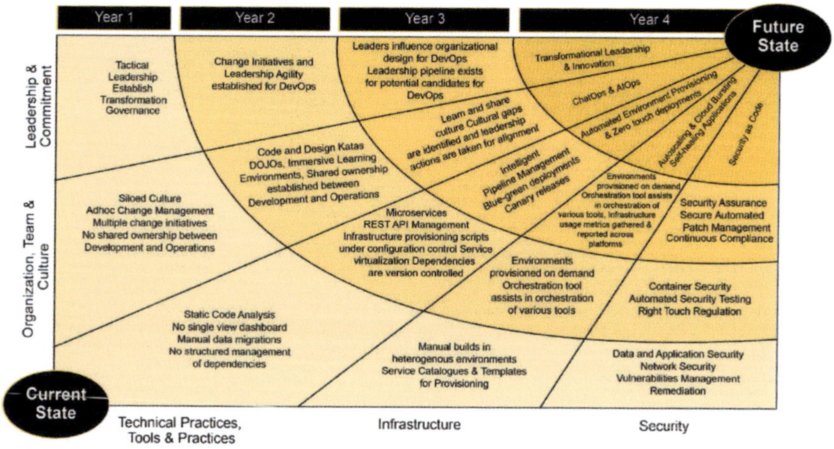

Points that you should take note of while planning out for transforming with DevOps

Create DevOps Teams from existing teams	Create DevOps transformation project plan	Assess the Culture and Readiness for DevOps	Define Funding Model and Transformation Budget	Invest on Training and Tools
Create Transformation Backlog	Define KPIs for Success	Select applications for Pilot	Baseline Pilot Application health	Govern and Manage Risk
Retrospect at regular intervals	Evangelize pilot wins across the organization	Define Rollout Strategy across organization	Empower Change Ambassadors and DevOps Champions across teams	Inspect, Adapt and Evolve

Once the transformation backlog items are identified, they are prioritized as a collaborative exercise with all the relevant stakeholders. The roadmap should also be treated as evolving and emergent to allow refinements from feedback acquired for continuous improvement. This will happen only when projects, programs and portfolios start adapting practices that influence team and organization behaviours.

The DevOps transformation plan, in addition to a DevOps transformation operating model or project plan, will ensure alignment between the organization and teams planning for transformation.

Developing a DevOps Progression Model

Assessments and maturity models have long been in close companionship. DevOps is a continuous journey and thus said, it may be difficult to associate a maturity level of DevOps for the entire organization due to the various nuances that impact an organization including organizational complexity, challenges, goals, change readiness, culture, priorities, leadership, infrastructure, governance structure and so on.

That said, what may be possible is judge where an organization is on an overall DevOps continuum on various disciplines and key practices. A sample progression model is crafted below for quick reference. Organizations may choose to create models based on their business context and how they choose to progress from one level to next.

DevOps Discipline	**Level 1**	**Level 2**	**Level 3**	**Level 4**	**Level 5**
	Initial	**Beginner**	**Intermediate**	**Advanced**	**Expert**
DevOps Mindset	* Tactical Leadership focused on problem solving * Avoidance of feedback and people connect * People lack trust and security in leadership * Leadership Agility is missing * No focus on innovation * Missing strategic alignment on the overall DevOps strategy, vision and goals * Development and Operations team operate as separate teams with a wall of confusion in between	* Organizational initiatives focus primarily on incremental improvements inside unit boundaries with little attention to stakeholder agility * More context-setting agility in terms of scoping initiatives and setting direction * Development and Operations teams work together with some sense of shared ownership	* Leadership establishes regular connect with people through floor walks and informal interactions * Open-door accessibility to leaders * Trust-based relationships are established and nurtured * Leaders participate and collaborate in driving pivotal conversations around people and organization growth needed for DevOps * Leaders are available to discuss challenges and implementation roadblocks on open forums with teams * Teams implement selected key practices to adopt DevOps with a common set of processes between Development and Operations	* Leaders are able to inspire and lead * A leadership pipeline exists for grooming potential candidates for DevOps * Leaders are able to influence change in the systems needed to influence the organizational design for DevOps	* Transformational Leadership that empowers and inspires individuals to lead * Leadership that nurtures personal visions of teams and influences strategic transformation objectives * Cross-functional DevOps teams work in a sustainable manner to deliver continuous value
DevOps Culture	* Siloed Culture * Change Management is adhoc and people dependent * Development and Operations do not share common goals and work as separate teams * Multiple tools used for the same purpose across multiple environments	* Isolated projects * Some elements of change management are being applied in isolated projects * Many different practices used inconsistently * Culture is identified but no actions are taken to align	* Well defined and structured approach for change management is being applied in multiple projects * Examples of best practices are evident * Culture is identified and gaps are explored with leadership assignment for action	* Organizational-wide standards and methods are implemented for change management * Culture is internalized across leadership and cascaded across teams and other organizational groups	* OCM as an organizational competency * OCM competency is valued and evident at all levels of the organization and is part of the organization's intellectual property and competitive edge * Continuous process improvement in place * Culture is aligned across the organization and tied to the way people are measured and rewarded

DevOps Discipline	Level 1	Level 2	Level 3	Level 4	Level 5
	Initial	**Beginner**	**Intermediate**	**Advanced**	**Expert**
Organizational Design for DevOps	* Dev and Ops are separate teams with no shared responsibilities * Inadequate governance for the DevOps goals * DevOps is the goal of few individuals and not the teams as a whole * No focus on competencies and awareness needed for DevOps	* Microservices driven architecture for new services developed * Domain Driven Design * REST API Management	* Immersive Learning * DOJOs	* ChatOps in place to facilitate problem solving and collaboration * Cloud Bursting and Autoscaling in place to facilitate surge demands for infrastructure capacity * Self-healing application design	* Performance Appraisals reflect the DevOps Culture * Self-organizing and Self-sustaining teams * Zero Intervention Production * AIOps for intelligent pipeline management
Continuous Learning	* No dedicated focus on learning * Ad hoc learning mechanisms	* Learning objectives are identified * Learning occurs in silos	* Code and Design Katas * DOJOs * Immersive Learning Environments	* Cross-pollination of learning through multiple forums * Learn and share culture	* Thought leadership through multiple forums
Continuous Integration, Delivery and Deployment	* Manual builds in heterogeneous environments * Separate build machines * Environments are manually provisioned * Manual data migrations without scripts	* Source control polling mechanism implemented * Build artifacts managed using source control * Build notifications configured * Standard process * Deployment scripts * Push button deployment to test environment * Scripted data migrations performed manually * Automated Integration Tests * Static code analysis	* Dependencies are version controlled * Versioning and tagging automated * Automated deployment to test environments * Automated changes to datastores * Rollback mechanism exist * Failover mechanism exists * Single standard process for all environments * Push button deployment to pre prod	* Triggered builds * Distributed builds on cluster * Push button deployment to production * Coordinated multitier deploymen * Blue-green deployment * Canary releases * Automated DB deployment * Promote VM / container for deployment	* Gated commits * Environments based on VMs * Zero touch (zero downtime) deploy to production
Continuous Monitoring	* No single view dashboard * Minimal monitoring with few OS level metrics * Static and Unit Tests done post-development	* Tool generated, custom reports with some metrics are available and visible * Mock for dependencies * Notifications configured	* Historical and cross function real time reports visible * Full quantitative metrics * Automated functional testing * Dynamic test coverage * Service Virtualization	* Cross-functional report trending including real time quality of service and pipeline metrics * IT for each commit * Automated performance and security testing * Semi-automated UAT	* Customizable cross-functional report analysis across organizational groups * Maximize UAT Automation * Dynamic self-service of analytics and information
DevOps Infrastructure	* Manually provisioned infrastructure * Provisioning errors cause delays in Dev and QA cycles * Multiple systems for environment provisioning	* Templates and service catalogs used for provisioning * Infrastructure Provisioning and deployment scripts are under source control	* Environments provisioned on demand * Orchestration tool assists in orchestration of various tools	* Infrastructure usage metrics gathered and reported for utilization * Services discovery and binding happens in PaaS * Managed environments end-to-end * Automated Secure Patching and upgrades are implemented	* Autoscaling and Cloud Bursting in place * Near instant deployment of changes (Push button deployments in place) * Zero downtime deployments * Self-healing application design facilitating zero intervention production
Continuous Security	* Data and Application Security * Network Security	* Automated Security Testing * Vulnerability Management * Remediation	* Container Security * Secure Automated Patch Management	* Right Touch Regulation * Continuous Compliance (at scale) * Security Assurance	* Security as Code
Points to Note					
For individual key practice areas, see detailed assessment scores and recommendations for improvement					
Not every discipline may be applicable to your business context. Applicable disciplines are determined during the scope discussion and pre assessment					

A Progression Model for DevOps in conjunction with a DevOps Transformation Roadmap will help to give direction to the transformation efforts of an organization gravitating towards DevOps.

Assessing ROI from DevOps

Assessing ROI from any change initiative has always been a priority item on every leader's agenda. That said, it has never been so straightforward or easy to estimate the ROI from any transformation or change. Similar is the case with a DevOps Transformation as well. Calculating ROI on your DevOps transformation right from coaching people to delivering smart business is no less than an enigma shrouded in mystery. Investments made to transform your organization with DevOps will certainly drive improvements and cost savings in the longer run, even if traditional short term ROI projections don't appear stellar.

Again, ROI for a transformation will never be a single number. It will be a combination of benefits - soft and hard that can be measured by quantitative metrics and qualitative assessments. For example, culture can be assessed through assessments and conversations, but cannot be quantified. At the same time, test automation coverage can be measured through KPIs and need not be subjective. Taking a holistic view of all these projections will give you a view of whether or not you are deriving value from your transformation.

Calculating ROI from a transformation means calculations at 2 levels - project (or program or application) and portfolio (or line of business or organization) level. Let's now dive into each of these levels and see what it means to project ROI here.

Another important point to be considered here is that it may be nearly impossible to attribute the entire ROI to purely DevOps in the presence of other change initiatives and improvement programs that may be ongoing in an organization.

What may be of interest to all stakeholders is to optimize the improvement efforts, keep workflows lean and nimble and achieve maximum benefits without compromising on the product quality or delivery timelines.

An improved ROI through adoption of immutable infrastructure, automated environment provisioning and improved enterprise collaboration may also result in a reduced Total Cost of Ownership (TCO).

ROI Projections at Project (rather Product) Level

In typical organizations, some of the costs and benefits will get apportioned across multiple buckets for purely financial accounting purposes and will get amortized over a longer period, not a few sprints. You may also choose to consider them as sunk costs for the ease of computation. For example, training costs and cost of enterprise licenses can be absorbed by the learning and development cost center or the delivery team or practice. The point to consider here is not who absorbs the cost, rather what is the cost per head and ultimately cost applicable to the project. 'Project' here ultimately refers to a product that is an independent revenue stream in product-based organizations and it also refers to projects created for operational purposes, as in the case of all system integrators.

Also, projected below are some of the metrics that might be relevant to your scenario. You can always decide on the metrics that matter most for ROI computation based on the dimensions of what product quality and business value mean to your project, customer and organization at large. The below list is not exhaustive and is drawn from past projects with whom I engaged on their transformation journeys. These were from various domains, geographies, industry segments and so the ones listed share some commonalities.

Costs

- o Measurable
  - o Competency building– Training, Self-learning, Hackathons and DOJOs
  - o Technology investments– Tooling, Infrastructure, Security and Replatforming programs
  - o Innovation-centric investments– Dedicated Innovation Sprints, Hackathons, participation in thought leadership forums and so on
  - o People investments– Rewards, recognitions and avenues to motivate teams and retain high performers
- o Non-measurable
  - o Reduced throughput due to new ways of working
  - o Learning curve Benefits
- o Measurable - Hard Benefits
  - o % Reduction in build failures per sprint
  - o % Reduction in code smells and vulnerabilities
  - o % Reusable components used in sprint

- % In-sprint automation
- % Testing effectiveness
- % UAT Automation
- Savings in fixing defects pre-prod
- Test Coverage
- % Technical debt introduced on new code
- % Reduction in technical debt on existing code
- Defects per sprint
- Improved Go-to-market (or deployment frequency)
- Reduction in lead time to deploy to production
- Improved change volume to production
- Change fail rate
- % Failed deployments
- Defect escape rate
- Number of security threats detected and defended
- MTTR (Mean Time To Recover/Restore)
- Fraud losses
- Penalties due to security breaches
- Net Promoter Score
- CSAT
- % of budget allocated for disruptive technologies and services
- % of new ideas that reach concept design
- Number of business days dedicated to Innovation activities each quarter

  - People engagement
  - Attrition index
- Non-measurable - Soft Benefits
  - Improved team and cross-functional collaboration
  - Improved code quality
  - Reduction in technical debt
  - Improved hygiene, discipline and governance
  - Improved ways of working through technical practices introduced
  - Innovation
  - Improved product security (reduction or avoidance of fraud losses and penalties due to security breaches)
  - Improved business value due to choice of technology platform, toolchain orchestration, architecture and other decisions stemming from the technical landscape
  - Speed of new technology implementation
  - Improved happiness quotient of people (both - teams and business)
  - Improved CAPEX through more services being hosted in cloud
  - Reduced revenue leakage and improved wallet share through new business opportunities with existing and new customers
  - Reduced cost of change
  - Improved customer experience
- Some ground rules
  - Baseline Measurements across Sprints
  - Measure Sprint-on-sprint

- o Focus on outcomes, not on outputs
- o Do not force fit targets on ROI aggressively in the initial few sprints; allow the team to adapt to the new ways of working and evolve
- o Do not superimpose traditional financial thinking and practices to achieve ROI targets quarter on quarter in the initial few quarters
- o Treat projects like products and transformation like a journey and build sustainability for long term vision over short-term gains

All these practices aim to influence the overall product or service delivery curve with DevOps and influence too directly or indirectly.

ROI Projections at Portfolio, Line of Business or Organizational Level

The same approach can be applied to derive the ROI projections from a portfolio with multiple applications and multiple releases every month. Projects may be bucketed by technology cluster, geography or domain to derive maximum value.

It may be important to also appreciate in hindsight some challenges encountered during ROI computation at portfolio, line of business or organization level. Some of these are listed below

- o Many organizations that are more financially driven choose to look at long term projections of ROI especially if shorter milestones do not reflect significant performance changes considering the time to acclimatize with the new ways of working that DevOps demands
- o Developing multi-year strategic roadmaps for products or service capabilities along with a view of financial projections is not easy for most organizations especially if they are highly data-driven. It may be a good idea to incorporate a certain degree of variability and uncertainty to factor the time to speed with DevOps.
- o Given the constantly changing DevOps technology landscape, it's very

difficult to quantify the benefit or risk — or how big the potential losses might be. Some other factors that influence ROI include but are not limited to the below

- Where you start your DevOps Transformation journey?
- What are your pilot projects that will be the ambassadors to catalyze DevOps in the organization?
- What are your top priorities or pain areas where you see adopting DevOps will make a difference
- Post-assessment, how does your organization sustain the transformation rigor and momentum?

To have a clear understanding of the benefits, it is a good idea to establish the current as a baseline and measure this post implementing DevOps at different points in time.

The benefits and challenges may vary with organization and business but if implemented with the right mindset and rigor, a DevOps Transformation transforms an organization for good overall.

So, this leaves me with a closing question:

Do you select and create ROI stories on assumptions and financial risk projections and try develop models that gets buy-in from leadership or do you rely on strategic vision,

leadership agility, execution capabilities and more importantly DevOps practices and mindset to evolve and adapt to dynamic and volatile market conditions and customer feedback to drive you to a digital future for your organization? I'm still thinking on this one but I believe the solution lies in establishing the right balance among vision, DevOps execution practices and lean financial methodologies.

How is DevOps for Digital different from DevOps for legacy systems?

DevOps for modern day digital applications differs from DevOps for legacy systems mainly in the way technology acceleration influences business landscape and demands disruption at the speed of DevOps.

- Digital applications dominate the budget in the space of rapid mobile application development, analytics and visualization to drive increased customer engagement and optimized business processes. Conversely, legacy applications are more focused on specific functionalities and are not so easy to integrate or scale up/down with growing business needs.
- Digital applications focus on leveraging the increasing spectrum of technologies in the most optimal manner to build up scalable and robust architecture and infrastructure. With legacy applications, decoupling modules might not be such an easy task.
- Modern day applications leverage technical practices like polyglot programming, configurable technology stack, immutable infrastructure and so on to meet runtime demands and offer a variety of choices at every layer of technology as compared to legacy applications that do not offer such flexibility.
- Rapid mobile application development is yet another factor that is driving DevOps to mobilize processes and rearchitect systems to influence revenues with a value-driven prioritization. Conversely, traditional development has always focused on a fixed set of outcomes with predefined priorities.
- Elastic infrastructure is yet another enabler of digital applications that can adapt to rapidly scale up or scale down based on fluctuating business demands. Anywhere mobile apps being used in both online and offline modes are an extended capability that business is ready to offer to complement such scenarios with an end objective to improve customer service or boost sales.
- IT Platformization is another key driver that differentiates the DevOps strategies for modern day applications. Development platforms are increasingly being used to define or complement existing architectures. There is a shift in focus to make enterprises more mobile and integrated with respect to platformizing their

approach to solution delivery, leadership and talent management. Orchestration of value at different business layers and creation of value at an enterprise level enables them to become digital leaders. Capitalizing on such platforms also gives them the benefit of leveraging in-built database structures, security workflows and enterprise data also enhancing time to market and usability.

- Emphasis on System Integration from Mobile to Back-End: Most businesses and customers nowadays prefer a custom mobile app for all their needs. These custom apps need integration with back-end legacy systems that have long cycle times spanning long real-time processes. Ensuring reusability of assets minimizing the overall approach to system integration of each such app is also a key driver to DevOps increasing the collaboration across multiple IT teams and business.
- Increase in Hybrid Integrations: Enterprises are increasingly shifting towards virtualization and adopting cloud infrastructure. With immutable infrastructure offering a spectrum of options from single cloud to multi-cloud, hybrid cloud integration is becoming the norm of modern-day enterprises. Implementing hybrid cloud infrastructure requires unified integration platforms orchestrated for enterprise capabilities. This is also a key driver to DevOps designing digital systems aimed at achieving competitive advantage and innovation providing true business value

Workforce Transformation for DevOps

Organizations that are embarking upon a transformation journey leveraging DevOps as an enabler spend huge amounts of money getting themselves assessed for readinessor adoption maturity, upgrading their technology stack and toolchains, overhauling and optimizing business processes and stacking talent pool in multiple areas that are needed with the new vision. While these are critical, many CIOs and business leaders have also realized that if they have to influence the customer experience by influencing employees in the way they serve customers, they must rethink and redefine or redesign their workforce transformation strategy for DevOps.

With growing digitization across industries, exploitation of digital technologies by a connected workforce with blurred boundaries across geographies is crucial to achieving competitive advantage. If this holds true, then what must be the factors to reflect for an effective workforce transformation for DevOps? This is crucial as it will also be part of the overall Transformation Roadmap in terms of identifying priorities and strategic solutions in the near, mid and long term.

Some of the factors that influence workforce transformation with DevOps include but are not limited to the following –

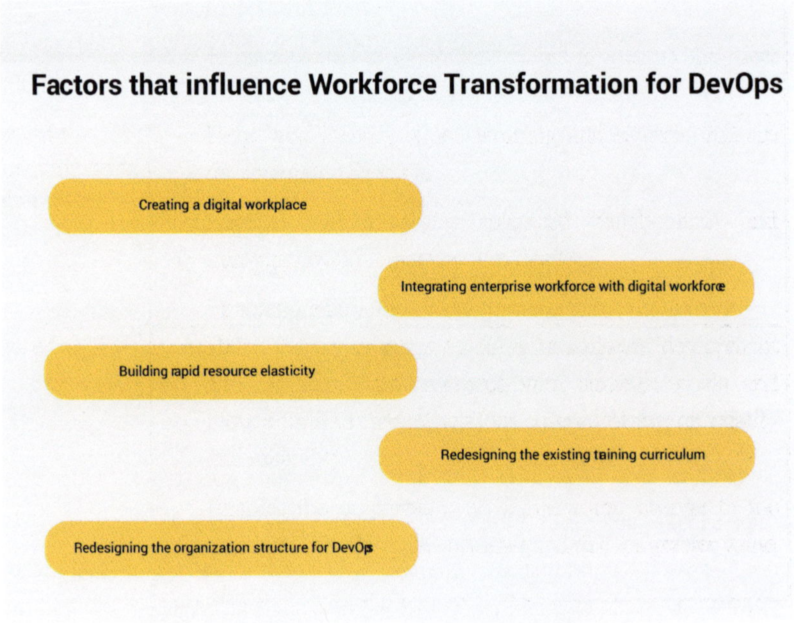

Factor	Influence
Creating a Digital Workplace	• It boosts team agility and better employee engagement through consumerization of the workplace • Enables teams to work more productively with a high degree of flexibility • Includes all kinds of devices that enable collaboration coupled with messaging services, video conferencing chatbots and immersive workspaces that retain the human connect
Leveraging Automation to build perfect co-existence of Enterprise Workforce and Digital Workforce	• Identify rule-driven, mundane tasks that are structured from a decision making perspective and repetitive in nature as early candidates for automation • Identifying tools that automatically modify code and test for security and compliance conditions with a high degree of test and functional coverage • Leveraging gamification to drive immersive learning as part of the overall DevOps adoption strategy • Leveraging RPA and AI for promoting intelligent deployments and zero intervention production with self healing systems • Typical areas that can benefit from RPA, AIOps and ChatOps include – o IT and Infrastructure Support o Customer Service and Support Desk o Data Migration and Management o Back Office Administration o Digital and Online Initiatives o Connecting Process Islands
Building Rapid Resource Elasticity	• Achieve on-demand infrastructure and environments and rapid resource elasticity • Focus on hiring the right talent in terms of complementing skills, competencies and mindset for DevOps • Focus on reskilling existing talent through promoting training, awareness, learning, hackathons and thought leadership in immersive environments
Redesign the existing Training Curriculum	• Redesign the entire learning roadmap to bridge the gap between current skills available and skills needed to embrace and implement DevOps • Get the necessary buy-in, funding and time approvals from management to ensure people attend and benefit from these programs and apply the learnings acquired to work • Track the giveback of these programs by practices implemented, benefits reaped and experience sharing sessions with Senior Management
Redesign organization structure for DevOps	• Co-create your DevOps Strategy with your human capital • Redesign roles and responsibility in alignment with DevOps needs • Build collaboration through a flat structure focusing importance on the role against titles in traditional structure • Build focus on generalist skills against the superhero mindset • Navigate talent hotspots and find change champions with a DevOps mindset to advocate the DevOps philosophy in the organization

Critical Success Factors for DevOps Transformation

Critical Success Factors for DevOps Transformation

It is a common belief amongst many people that DevOps cannot be implemented for long running applications or legacy systems and that startups are the best fit. But if you take a look at some of the exceptional examples of implementations of DevOps with large organizations like Amazon, Netflix, Facebook, etc., it is evident that they have achieved this despite their significant size and business critical legacy systems.

In my view, implementing DevOps in existing applications and brownfield applications has a significant advantage because most such applications have an already identified gap between their performance throughput and customer expectations. Such applications can be analyzed for reduction of technical debt or enhancement of deployment cycle times through automation for existing product features.

Handling legacy architecture and re-architecting newer services that integrate with the enterprise elephant and don't create surprise breaks takes time to develop confidence.

Sometimes, applications may throw intermittent errors that are not easy to trace from the perspective of mapping them to the root cause. Is the error due to a change introduced in the toolchain integration or was it a hidden error inherent in the system that just got surfaced now? Have I lifted and shifted my data centers in a secure and optimum manner? Is my approach still sub-optimal? These and many more questions may be points that drive your overall approach to transformation.

All these can be brownie points for your DevOps initiative with brownfield services or products. Although more challenging yet it will be more rewarding, convincing, encouraging and impactful at your organization.

From a plethora of factors that influence transformation success or failure, it may be worthwhile to do some retrospection on few that are critical to such an endeavor. Successful organizations share quite a few commonalities when it comes to transforming with DevOps leveraging technology frontiers. Listed below are some of them from my experience.

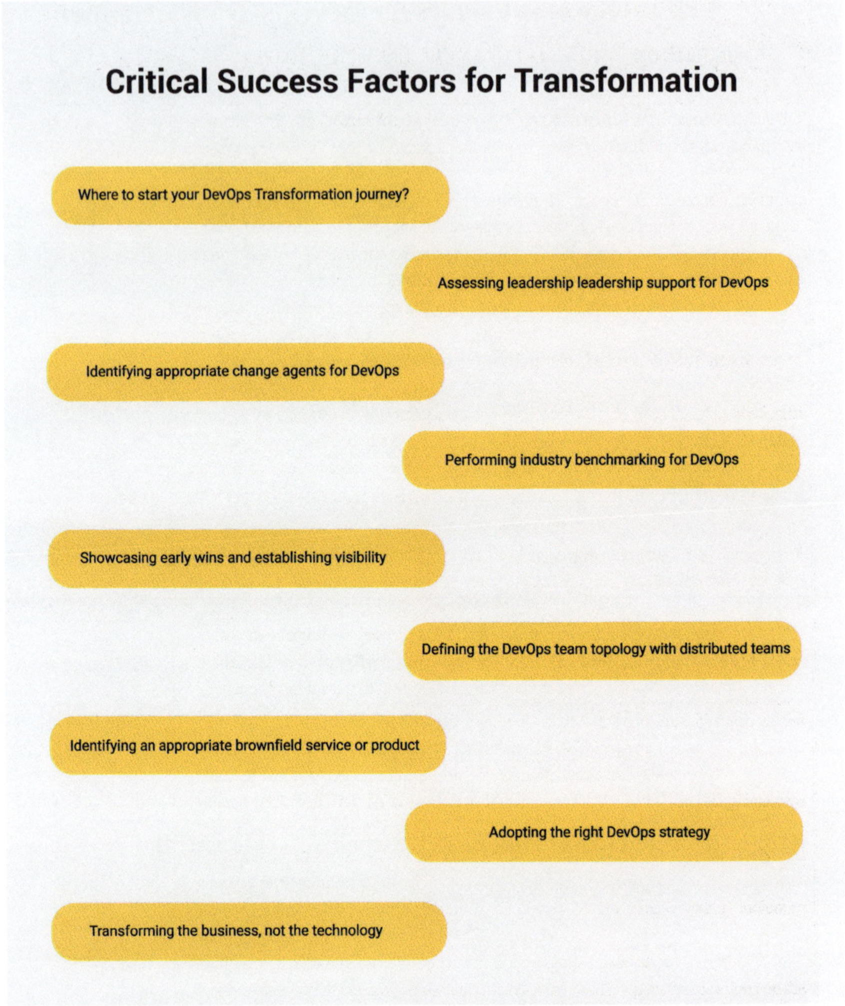

CSF	Influence on DevOps Transformation
Where to start your DevOps Transformation journey?	• Pilot success is vital to the success of organizational transformation • Right projects, early wins, ruthless retrospectives, technology stack of pilot and tangible improvements are important • Success to be evangelized across organization to get buy-in from all

CSF	Influence on DevOps Transformation
Assessing leadership and gauging leadership support for DevOps	• Assessing leadership agility for DevOps is crucial to understanding their commitment and support for DevOps • Understanding leadership strategies to manage change in a multi-speed environment influencing organization redesign for DevOps is crucial to assessment • Are leaders open to fostering a culture to innovate? Are they willing to take the risks to fail early with a long term view to succeed early? • Is innovation and disruption merely a number game or is it trickled through all the layers of organization in true spirit? • How lean and decentralized is the overall governance process and what is the role of leadership in empowering people to adopt and transform with DevOps? • Are there any Behavioural patterns emerging from assessment conversations and focus group audits that demonstrate alignment of leadership vision to DevOps strategy? • A 12-factor assessment (shown in following figure) of individual leadership profiles assessed during the DevOps Assessment may be extrapolated statistically to draw the median scores that assess if leadership behaviours are aligned to DevOps and the overall personality of the organization
Identifying appropriate change agents for DevOps	• Focused hiring of DevOps coaches and technologists with complementary T-shaped skills across the DevOps Program • Identification of change agents who possess an active mix of technical skills, hands-on implementation experience with CI-CD leveraging multiple tools, automation focus, cloud infrastructure knowledge, change management competencies, behavioural traits and a DevOps mindset • Grooming of change agents to embrace the culture and readiness to change is imperative to keep them continuously abreast with evolving technological landscape • Designing immersive learning experiences with newer ways of continuous learning leveraging these change catalysts • A 17-factor assessment (shown in following figure) of individual change agent profiles assessed during the DevOps Assessment may be extrapolated statistically to draw the median scores that assess if change agents are aligned to DevOps and whethe they are exhibiting the right behaviours to influence change
Performing industry benchmarking for DevOps	• Industry benchmarking has always been a way to drive targets in the organization; however, it may not be applicable to set targets for metrics based on competitor outcomes or goals • What may be of interest and applicability is an understanding of the organization's use case and business case for DevOps and conducting a focused industry study leveraging research analyst groups that can provide inputs feeding into the organization's DevOps strategy
Focussing on showcasing early wins and establishing visibility	• Demonstrating quick and early wins to prove business value from transformation to critics and naysayers • Demonstrating improved customer satisfaction and revenues • Replicating these wins and improvements in other pockets of the organization

CSF	Influence on DevOps Transformation
DevOps team topology with distributed teams	• Piloting with co-located teams is always a preferential way of executing, but the reality of success from business transformation lies in the scalability of the solution to extend to distributed teams • It may be a good idea to explore the benefits that elastic infrastructure offers for distributed teams and workloads. Containers may be a good option here for most applications embracing virtualization • Ensuring development to operations handoffs happen in the same geography and at least one or more developers are part of the operations team and vice-versa where the application has to be supported • DevOps may help you iteratively develop such applications which will then get hosted in the cloud • Usage of sandboxes may benefit as they will enable you to develop your application in such a manner that both the application and infrastructure appear the same irrespective of being accessed from development lab, testing lab, production data center or any other environment

Identifying an appropriate brownfield service or product	• Prefer brownfield product or service over greenfield
	• Advantages of brownfield product or service include the following
	  • Most of these applications are already running in production and so any transformation here is highly rewarding
	  • Buy-in is higher because these are business critical application
	  • Most of these have high technical debt with very less test automation and hence create a significant opportunity for improvement

Adopting the right DevOps strategy	• Adopt the right adoption strategies for DevOps that drive culture changes in the organization with transformational leadership and technical acumen • Have buy-in from senior management for transformation initiatives • Ensure leadership priorities are aligned to influence DevOps leveraging business technology to its best • Nurture a culture that is willing to embrace change with a fail fast, fail early and succeed early mindset • Engage multiple and diverse teams in all phases of the transformation including strategy, planning, and design • Build a community of change ambassadors across the organization • Perform succession planning and grooming of people and keep their aspirations on the forefront of transformation agenda
Transforming the business, not the technology	• Encourage innovation and build a technology blueprint that will deliver strategic and tactical value • Technology should be integrated with business and not looked at in isolation to harness the maximum benefit of disruption • Maintain the existing platforms while also exploring the emergent platforms and create an enterprise toolchain best suited to business needs • Focus on eliminating manual workflows and free up the bandwidth of people for more creativity and business improvements

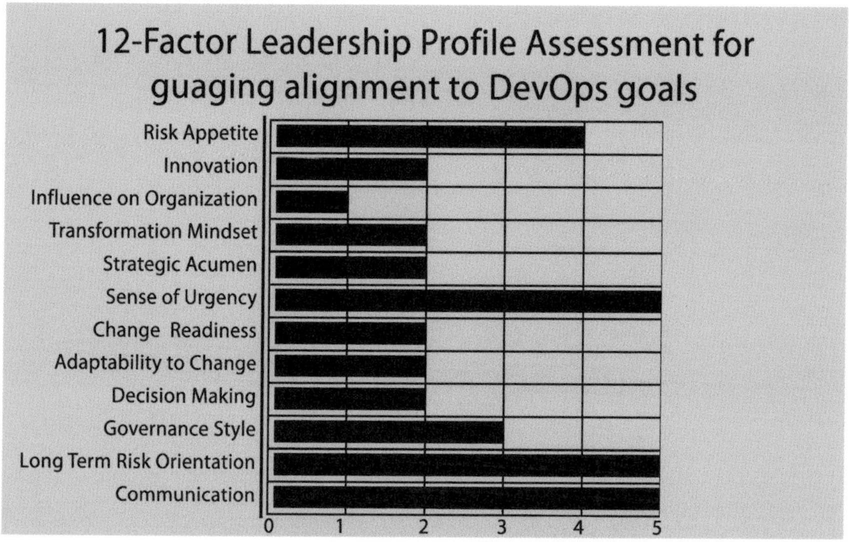
12-Factor Leadership Profile Assessment for guaging alignment to DevOps goals
Risk Appetite
Innovation
Influence on Organization
Transformation Mindset
Strategic Acumen
Sense of Urgency
Change Readiness
Adaptability to Change
Decision Making
Governance Style
Long Term Risk Orientation
Communication
0
1
2
3
4
5

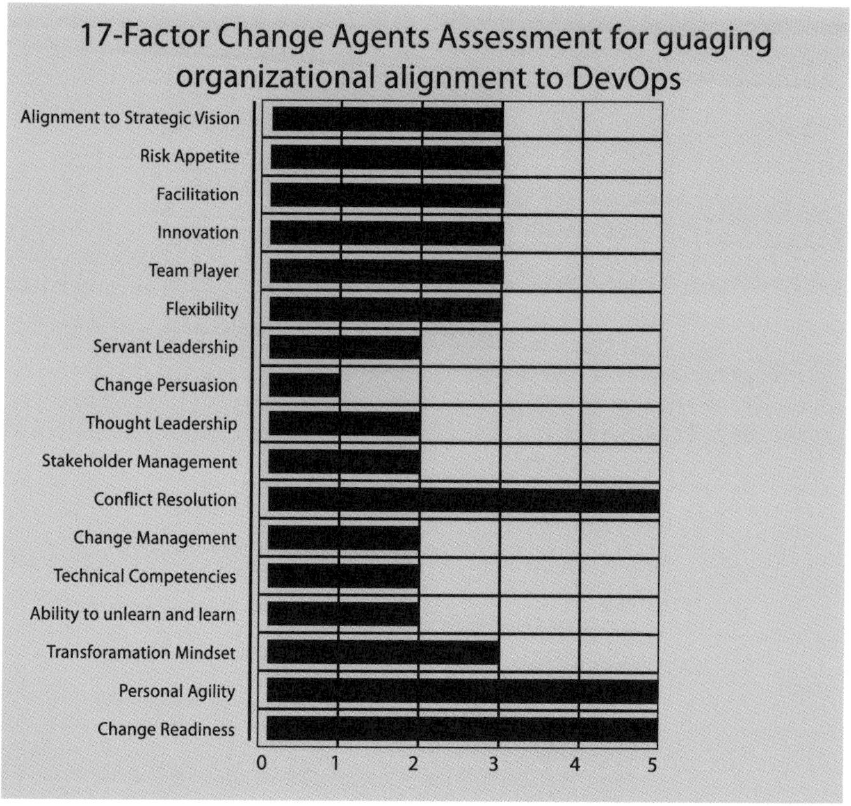
17-Factor Change Agents Assessment for guaging organizational alignment to DevOps
Alignment to Strategic Vision
Risk Appetite
Facilitation
Innovation
Team Player
Flexibility
Servant Leadership
Change Persuasion
Thought Leadership
Stakeholder Management
Conflict Resolution
Change Management
Technical Competencies
Ability to unlearn and learn
Transforamation Mindset
Personal Agility
Change Readiness
0
1
2
3
4
5

The Secret Sauce to Successful DevOps Transformation

An impactful start and early wins are imperative to a successful transformation. It is recommended that you pick your lighthouse projects judiciously. Equally critical is your DevOps team that is executing this pilot. You need strong ambassadors of change to catalyze transformation. People with an open-minded and growth mindset who are ready to learn and adapt to the newer ways of working.

It may not be with the time to select conservative minds who are doubtful if DevOps would bring the intended benefits. Such projects should also be cross-functional in nature, involve different capabilities and cut across the organization to harvest maximum benefits. The pilot also has to be a dedicated effort and people working on the pilot cannot be pulled onto other commitments ad hoc. This comes with an appropriate buy-in for DevOps. One or two teams are sufficient to start a pilot. Leveraging all these and any other strategic priorities of the organization, you may identify a brownfield service or product that best matches the selection criteria for the pilot.

Securing quick wins is not enough. You should be able to broadcast these at the right forums to make more people aware of the benefits that DevOps harbingers. Sound boarding success stories leveraging pilot adopters may be a good idea to introduce change catalysis throughout the organization. This will facilitate traction towards more adopters generating higher trust in DevOps in the organization.

Once more and more people see visible and measurable benefits, it is relatively easier to get support, sponsorship and attention from management too.

Conclusion

Conclusion

To ensure that your DevOps transformation is successful, identify a team that is composed of champions of change who will advocate and propagate it and strongly communicate progress. It is also imperative to include senior management from IT and operations plus change champions from other business enabling functions to drive business outcomes collaboratively. The underlying assumption here is that these champions are empowered to build an ecosystem of trust which will have a safety net to embrace failures from experimentation, risk and new ways of working. The DevOps vision for continuous delivery and continuous deployment should be aligned with the strategic vision. A DevOps Assessment helps you identify these gaps in alignment and enables you to better reposition your organization to be designed for DevOps.

We have seen in the earlier pages that a DevOps Assessment of an organization is a holistic dip stick from the perspectives of leadership organization culture, technical practices, infrastructure and security. Post Assessment, an organization can choose to embark on a DevOps journey with a more structured transformation roadmap.

The challenges encountered in implementing DevOps will vary from organization to organization based on business context. But to know the specific challenges of your organization and what is it that needs to change from a DevOps perspective, you will need to assess for DevOps. I am strictly not of the opinion that DevOps cannot be implemented in organizations that have legacy systems running their core business. In fact, most of my experience has spanned around banking and financial services institutions that have their core systems all in legacy. While it is hard to decouple such systems, it is not impossible. Certain elements of such systems will prove as an impediment to build in end-to-end automation and continuous delivery or deployment at the drop of a hat. Certain legacy systems are so architected that integrating services leveraging REST APIs may not be seemingly simple and technically feasible. Such systems should be isolated and adapted to change more on a case to case basis.

What is more important is whether the organization culturally is open to embrace a certain degree of architectural change even if the anticipated rate of change is slow. Monolithic architecture will slow down the pace of DevOps because a lot of applications have not been built with a service-oriented architecture strategy, but it is important to deliberate on how these applications will be integrated with the overall transformation strategy.

DevOps has evolved organically in most organizations and there has been an evergrowing number of tools and utilities that are aimed at facilitating implementation ease. Due to this, it will not be a surprise if we find two working next to each other separated by different tools which again translates to communication breaks and silos.

Assessing for enterprise tooling and automation capabilities also emphasizes the fact that rather than mandating a standardized toolset across all teams, it may be worthwhile to allow the flexibility of multiple teams leverage a loosely-coupled DevOps toolchain that they feel most appropriate and one which facilitates end-to-end communication and collaboration channels and also integrates with the existing set of tools in the organization.

An assessment may also give you recommendations on some of the below aspects towards architecting your toolchains.

- **Integrated toolchains** that are hosted on the cloud and can be easy to consume. Such tools not only integrate with each other but also integrate with the enterprise toolsuite. They can complement your existing toolchain and help adapt to the changing needs of the enterprise
- **Visualization** and **Analytics** is another powerful outcome from toolchain assessments. They enable visualizing real-time data and metrics that give a complete view of pipeline data at every stage of the lifecycle.
- **Automated DevOps Pipelines:** Assessments provide recommendations on technical practices that are best suited for DevOps and enable pattern identification for building cloud-specific automation in a DevOps pipeline
- **Multi/Hybrid Cloud full spectrum DevOps:** With hybrid cloud implementations

becoming the norm of enterprises, architects must account for the differences in platforms so that the right native features can be leveraged without negatively impacting the automation and productivity gains anticipated from DevOps

An organizational transformation always occurs while keeping in mind the need to keep business running while making necessary changes to revamp and transform. Without getting into a full-scale architectural revolution, you may still need to think on what kind of services can be independently introduced as microservices, what components from existing systems can be fully automated and so on. Siebel is one such example where you can fully automate the deployments. That creates bandwidth for the operations team to concentrate on other elements and areas of focus for DevOps that are more challenging to embrace.

One critical point here is to ensure all automation solutions have integrations architected to suit SAP, Siebel, Oracle and similar systems and this facilitates interaction ease when it comes to talking with legacy systems resident in some of the applications selected for implementing DevOps. Doing so will facilitate legacy systems to be enablers rather than impediments of change that we wish to bring to realize the full potential of DevOps.

No team can work in a vacuum and deliver successful projects. Making key decisions about features, functionality and benefits, engaging the customer on the entire journey, setting up the ecosystem for DevOps in the Customer's organization landscape while constantly schedules, approaches in increments and iterations all require a DevOps mindset to think how to break complex solutions into smaller sizeable potentially shippable product increments (PSPIs) which together will integrate to build the final product or solution.

A transformation of any sort is never easy or quick. And a DevOps transformation is no exception. In today's customer-centric and fast-paced era organizations cannot afford the luxury of transforming in just a few areas and letting the rest go. Organizations must walk the digital journey together. A DevOps Assessment helps them get this view of where they stand as an organization with respect to the changing needs of technology and business landscape in alignment with what is their future strategy. Technology leaders have long realized that transforming organizations embracing DevOps practices and automation to streamline application delivery can help establish a winning proposition in the digital age.

List of Abbreviations	
Abbreviation	**Expanded Form**
A/B	Alpha / Beta
AI	Artificial Intelligence
API	Application Program Interface
ATDD	Acceptance Test Driven Development
BAU	Business As Usual
BDD	Behaviour Driven Development
BI	Business Intelligence
CAPEX	Capital Expenditure
CEO	Chief Executive Officer
CI-CD	Continuous Integration Continuous Delivery
CIO	Chief Information Officer
CMM	Capability Maturity Model
CMMI	Capability Maturity Model Integration
CoE	Centre of Excellence
COTS	Commercial Off-The-Shelf
CSAT	Customer Satisfaction
CSF	Critical Success Factor
CTO	Chief Technology Officer
DAST	Dynamic Application Security Testing
DB	Database
DBA	Database Administrator

List of Abbreviations	
Abbreviation	**Expanded Form**
DIY	Do It Yourself
DoS	Denial of Service
FT	Functional Testing
GDPR	General Data Protection Regulation
HR	Human Resources
IaC	Infrastructure as Code
IAST	Interactive Application Security Testing
IE	Immersive Environment
IT	Information Technology
JEDI	Just Enough Design Initially
JSON	JavaScript Object Notation
KPI	Key Performance Indicator
KRA	Key Responsibility Area
MITM	Man In The Middle
ML	Machine Learning
MOOC	Massive Open Online Course
MSA	Master Services Agreement
MTBF	Mean Time Between Failures
MTTR	Mean Time To Recover
NPS	Net Promoter Score
OCM	Organizational Change Management

List of Abbreviations	
Abbreviation	**Expanded Form**
OPEX	Operational Expenditure
OS	Operating System
OSNA	Objective Score Not Applicable
PAAS	Platform As A Service
PLM	Product Lifecycle Management
POC	Proof of Concept
POV	Point of View
PSPI	Potentially Shippable Product Increment
QA	Quality Assurance
RACI	Responsible Accountable Consulted Informed
RASP	Runtime Application Security Performance
REST API	Representational State Transfer Application Program Interface
ROI	Return on Investment
RPO	Recovery Point Objective
SAST	Static Application Security Testing
SCM	Source Code Management
SDLC	Software Development Lifecycle
SDN	Software Defined Networking
SIG	Special Interest Group
SLA	Service Level Agreement
SI	System Integration

List of Abbreviations	
Abbreviation	**Expanded Form**
SIT	System Integration Testing
SoD	Separation of Duties
SOW	Statement of Work
SSA	Software Security Assurance
SVN	Subversion
TCO	Total Cost of Ownership
TDD	Test Driven Development
TLM	Technology Lifecycle Management
UAT	User Acceptance Testing
UT	Unit testing
VM	Virtual Machine
VSS	Visual Source Safe
VUCA	Volatile, Uncertain, Complex, Ambiguous
WSJF	Weighted Shortest Job First

Bibliography

Books referred to -

1. The Phoenix Project: Gene Kim , Kevin Behr and George Spafford
2. Accelerate: Gene Kim, Nicole Forsgren
3. The Lean Startup: Eric Ries
4. Business Model Generation: Alex Osterwalder and Dr. Yves Pigneur
5. The Design Thinking Playbook: Michael Lewrick
6. The Heart of Change: John Kotter
7. Our Iceberg is Melting: John Kotter and Holger Rathgeber
8. Disciplined Agile Delivery: Scott W. Ambler and Mark Lines
9. Choose Your WoW: Scott W. Ambler and Mark Lines
10. The Execution Factor: Kim Perell
11. DevOps for Serverless Architectures: Shashikant Bangera
12. Enterprise Agility: Sunil Mundra
13. Android Security Essentials: Pragati Ogal Rai
14. From Team Player to Team Leader: Mandar Kulkarni
15. Mindset: Carol S. Dweck
16. The 5 AM Club: Robin Sharma
17. Coaching Agile Teams: Lyssa Adkins
18. Product Roadmaps Relaunched: C. Todd Lombardo, Michael Connors CSC, Bruce McCarthy and Evan Ryan
19. Unlocking Agility: Jorgen Hesselberg

Other Websites and Links referred to -

Pilot Project Selection

- *https://blog.flux7.com/devops-adoption-7-lessons-for-a-successful-devops-pilot*
- *https://devops-research.com/assets/devops_scorecard.pdf*

Scriptless Automation and Jobs-as-Code

- *https://searchitoperations.techtarget.com/tip/Conduct-an-impartial-DevOps-assessment-for-your-organization#commenting*

Self-healing

- *https://technologyconversations.com/2016/01/26/self-healing-systems/*
- *https://docs.microsoft.com/en-us/azure/architecture/guide/design-principles/self-healing*

Immutable Infrastructure

- *https://www.digitalocean.com/community/tutorials/what-is-immutable-infrastructure*

Microservices

- *https://www.ibm.com/cloud/garage/architectures/devOpsArchitecture*

DevSecOps

- *http://www.itbriefcase.net/where-does-security-fit-in-devops*
- *https://www.beyondtrust.com/blog/entry/devops-security-best-practices*
- *https://simpleprogrammer.com/security-code-secure-devops/*
- *https://www.techopedia.com/definition/13567/application-security*
- *http://www.change-management.com/ecmlab/ECM-Lab-Preread-M-Model.pdf*

Right-touch Regulation

- *https://www.professionalstandards.org.uk/docs/default-source/publications/thought-paper/right-touch-regulation-2015*
- *https://www.professionalstandards.org.uk/what-we-do/improving-regulation/right-touch-regulation*

Security Assurance

- *https://www.structured.com/wp-content/uploads/2016/08/Solution-Story-Security-Assurance.pdf*

DevOps Progression Model

- *https://www.nebbiatech.com/2018/08/09/assessing-your-devops-capability-level-some-lessons-learned/#post/0*

Agile Transformation Roadmap

- *https://www.castsoftware.com/research-labs/agile-transformation-roadmap*
- *https://www.gruntwork.io/devops-checklist/*

Cloud Bursting

- *https://www.aviatrix.com/blog/making-cloud-bursting-work-hybrid-cloud-environment/*
- *https://searchcloudcomputing.techtarget.com/definition/cloud-bursting*
- *https://www.linkedin.com/pulse/checklist-build-devops-organization-thomas-theakanath/*

How DevOps for digital is different from DevOps for Legacy?

- *https://enterprisersproject.com/article/2015/12/digital-transformation-priorities-CIOs-2016*
- *https://www.softwaretestinghelp.com/tools/top-40-static-code-analysis-tools/*

How to Create a Transformation Roadmap?

- *http://hrishikeshkarekar.com/2014/10/cost-delay-economic-model-decision-making/*
- *https://www.scaledagileframework.com/wsjf/*

Acknowledgments

This book is a perfect example of incremental and emergent design. It is built on the product backlog of my dreams and desires to share my experiences acquired across these years with my dear readers.

I am immensely grateful that this book is in your hands. My deep hope is that it serves the full expression of your strategic objectives and brings the desired transformation rigour, which is vital for DevOps.

But it would have been impossible to put this across had it not been the mentors who groomed me during this entire sojourn. In no particular order, I would like to elicit their names as a token of gratitude.

A deep gratitude and love to my parents – Narayandas and Kalpana Naidu who have always nurtured the passion to write as a child and kept grooming and encouraging that all through the years till today. The pride I have seen in their eyes for every single and small win kept the fire within me burning to write this book. My spouse Hari, mom-in-law Kamalakumari, brother and sister-in-law Amit and Ankita and most importantly my tiny tots – Tanushri and Mrithul, each of them enabled me to finish this book. Thank you, my precious gems, for keeping up with my crazy schedules to bring this out..

I have given my very best to create this book for you. Writing this section gives me a deep sense of happiness combined with gratitude as it gives a sense of completion of this manuscript. And I greatly thank all the very great mentors who globally supported me in putting this across.

In no order of preference, I would like to thank all my mentors and some close friends (names placed in alphabetical order of first name). Your invaluable insightsand guidance cannot be genuinely thanked enough.

1. Abhay Kale
2. Abhaya Gupta
3. Akhil Bhansali
4. Altaf Husein Vohra
5. Anil Kumar
6. Anirban Bose
7. Arun Daswani
8. Ashutosh Bhatawadekar
9. Dhiraj Sinha
10. Dilip Kulkarni
11. Geetanjali Khatri
12. Hrishikesh Karekar
13. Krishnamurthy Voora
14. Madan Upadhyay
15. Mahesh Raut
16. Malolan Sarangapani
17. Manish Joshi
18. Manish Mehta
19. Manish Nashine
20. Manushree Singh
21. Masa K Maeda
22. Mike Fidgeon
23. Neha Punather
24. Nilesh Vaidya
25. Padmini Nidumolu
26. Paul Wilkinson
27. Prachi Saraph
28. Prakash Punnekat
29. Ramesh Venugopalan
30. Robin Sharma
31. Sanjay Kumar Mandal
32. Sanjeev Kulkarni
33. Satyajit Mohanty
34. Scott W. Ambler
35. Sonal Drone
36. T N Mukundan
37. Thomas Stiehm
38. Tracy Bridenbaugh
39. Umesh Jain
40. Vikas Uppal
41. Vipin Srivastava
42. Virat Bhartiya

Immense gratitude goes to the fantastic team at Adhyyan Books who did such a great job with editing, publishing and promoting this book. All their artful efforts and creative design that helped me get this masterpiece on paper. Their professionalism, care, and support made the "last mile" so much easier. Thanks! Holding the galley copy is akin to holding your baby when you first become a parent.

Saying thank you starts with Hrishikesh Karekar, my mentor and coach who helped me put my best foot forward and finish this book in particularly difficult times. There is so much to learn from you Hrishi. Thank you so much.

Special thanks to Nilesh Vaidya, who did a detailed review of the book from the perspective of enabling strategic leaders to derive maximum value. Nilesh– thank you for taking time off your multiple commitments and sharing your feedback that enabled me to get this final version out.

A big thanks to Abhaya Gupta, Krishnamurthy Voora and Geetanjali Khatri for sparing time to walkthrough and providing a treasure-trove of insights that enriched the earlier version to the present form you hold.

Special thanks to Manish Joshi, Manish Mehta, Dhiraj Sinha, Neha Punather, Manushree Singh, Ramesh Venugopalan, Dilip Kulkarni, Altafhusein Vohra and Virat Bhartiya for doing a detailed review and sharing some immensely valuable examples and very selective feedback that enriched the value of content that represents the present form of the book.

A big thanks to Vipin Srivastava who spent countless hours to review chapter by chapter for many months together since the inception of this book and gave me very pragmatic feedback that reflects in the version you hold. Vipin– thank you for walking with me and guiding me throughout this project.

Special thanks to Umesh Jain and Sonal Drone for brainstorming and technical proofreading all through the book from inception to the final version

Special thanks to Prakash Punnekat for mentoring me through both the books and on various areas that stirred my spirits to get this out live. No words can be sufficient to express my gratitude to you, Prakash.

Last but not the least, the many practitioners, peers, friends and colleagues who actively debated with me on multiple ideas, I cannot thank you enough for enabling me to shape my perspectives and propelling the writer's force in me to get the adrenaline rush in print. To all those mentioned and missing, a big thank you for all your support.

Happy Reading!

Endorsements

The DevOps Assessment Playbook provides a simple yet holistic approach for conducting assessments for any enterprise that is planning to embark on the DevOps journey. Written from a pure practitioner perspective, it gets headfirst into assessment by providing a comprehensive set of questions that are the heart of all interview conversations without being prescriptive and yet with a fine attention to details. Read this to retrospect where you are in your DevOps transformation and what areas you may need to pay special attention to while architecting your DevOps strategy. A definite read for all CIOs and business leaders who plan to embark this journey.

Abhaya Gupta, Executive Vice President, Capgemini

Urmila provides a compelling business case to adopt DevOps through "The DevOps Assessment Playbook". Coming from a practitioner supported by her in-depth understanding of technology and agile methods, through this book she provides practical insights and steps to be undertaken on how to conduct assessments, analyze and build road maps for DevOps adoption. The book is very well organized and easy to read making it a quick reference guide for any organization.

Krishnamurthy Voora, Executive Vice President, Capgemini

The DevOps Assessment Playbook is a compelling reference that I foresee a wide variety of Technology organizations benefitting from in their DevOps journey. An extremely methodical primer for any leader embarking on the DevOps journey to retrospect on their readiness for DevOps and to achieve progression to the next level on a continuous improvement continuum Urmila has done a brilliant job in covering the different aspects of Assessment and Transformation such as providing recommendations on crafting a DevOps Transformation Roadmap, determining ROI from your Transformation initiative, planning the workforce transformation needed for DevOps and exploring the nuances of one such transformation from legacy to digital. All in all, an impressive effort with multiple takeaways for every strategy consultant and business leader who wants to transform the organization landscape with DevOps.

Geetanjali Khatri, Executive Vice President, Capgemini

Urmila has done a marvelous job in putting the DevOps Assessment Playbook, this is a well thought and researched product and is a one-stop shop for any organization, who want to embark the DevOps journey. This book is perfect guide to do the DevOps assessment. It is very well organized, easy to read and a step by step guide for DevOps assessment.

Vipin Srivastava, Director, Capgemini

This book is very impressive. Well-structured and lined up thoughts showcases the author's immeasurable efforts and ground level experience. Her research and analysis have given a wider view on DevOps assessment. Definitely a positive light for leaders in DevOps journey.

Dilip Kulkarni, Director, Capgemini

The author of DevOps Assessment Playbook uses the experience and deep industry research to explain how enabling DevOps is key to engaging the workforce of the future. If you're looking for ideas on how to do that, this book will get you started.

Altafhusein Vohra, Director, Capgemini

A refreshing take on DevOps from a seasoned practitioner who brings in practical insights that will be immensely useful to anyone embarking on the assessment journey. While the content is fairly detailed, the treatment is light and easy to read, unencumbered of disinteresting theory. The book is honest in its intent and delivers genuine value to readers who are looking to design DevOps in their enterprises in a structured manner.

Virat Bhartiya, Senior Director, Capgemini

In the DevOps journey, it is very important to keep on checking periodically if you are headed in the right direction. And for that, if you get a guide who has undertaken the journey before and knows how to navigate you without overwhelming you, your probability of success increases significantly. Urmila has done a wonderful job in making that guide available to you. It is practical yet provides new insights. Detailed, yet easy to follow. Keep this as your reference material and you will have the assurance that you are headed in the right direction.

Dhiraj Sinha, Vice President, Capgemini

The DevOps Assessment Playbook provides guidance for assessing the organizational readiness for DevOps and creating organizational cultures and ecosystems to support the workforce transformation for DevOps. CIOs can harness the key practices proposed in this guide to co-create a true DevOps organization and influence organizational redesign. I like the way Security has been given a cornerstone place in the entire assessment schema that emphasizes very well that it cannot be an afterthought.

This book is a must-have resource for all DevOps strategy consultants and all business leaders who know that the key to their organizations' success in today's complex global economy is the transformation of their human capital.

Urmila beautifully illustrates the complex cognitive blend of organizational, business and technical competencies needed to navigate successfully in continuously changing cross-cultural business and technology landscape. From an overview of the soft skills and behaviours needed to achieve mindset transformation, to technical excellence in design approaches, to workforce transformation for DevOps, to what it takes to create Security ingrained as part of the overall DevOps culture. This work is an invaluable guide for organizational leaders who can achieve success with successful implementation of DevOps within their organization.

Manish Mehta, Vice President, Capgemini

Urmila has put together an outstanding piece of work. She has structured her thoughts and the concepts really well, kept it simple and interesting at the same time. She has put her experience on paper which will work as a guide and a reference to keep you on the right track. This is impressive and powerful with multiple takeaways.

Manushree Singh, Director, Capgemini

The author is a distinguished IT professional with a diverse spectrum of experiences in the IT industry including IT service companies and captives – primarily in the banking captive space making her one of the key contributors to banking IT. In todays' ever-changing world of dynamic economic environments, continuously evolving technologies and transforming societies – the author works at the center of these changes. Her contribution to the IT industry is distinguished by her capability to use her insightful knowledge in technology, human behaviours and ability to network – to make seamless deliveries happen in a cost-effective manner that are extremely high in quality. Her ability to integrate her technical knowledge to construct heterogeneous solutions that are highly scalable, adaptive and robust – makes her an illustrious consultant.

Umesh Jain, Vice President, Deutsche Bank Group

As a consulting practitioner in IT led business transformations, I find this book an excellent practical guide for organizations wanting to imbibe DevOps principles. Even with little experience on the subject, the book provides the reader steps to undertake assessments in a very structured manner keeping in mind varying contexts and most importantly objective measurements on various dimensions. I liked the focus on finer aspects of the book such as: "continuous improvement", "where to start", "measurement of areas as different levels".

Sonal Drone, Managing Consultant, IBM

A lot has been written about various aspects of DevOps but nowhere else I have seen the depth and practice brought to light so intelligently and comprehensively as here. A must-have collection on every strategic leader's toolkit for DevOps transformation.

Manish Nashine, Director, Dun and Bradstreet

Praise for "The DevOps Assessment Playbook". It is a powerful book providing you with the necessary information and tools to successfully progress your journey to create your DevOps Transformation. An incredible guide to transforming your DevOps.

Tracy Bridenbaugh, CEO and Digital Transformation Leader,

Tracy Bridenbaugh and Associates

This book is a comprehensive and well-structured book on how to perform effective DevOps assessments which will be handy reference material for DevOps Consultants and Architects who are looking to transform their Enterprise Software Development and Implementation practices in line with the current Industry trend. Urmila is a well-known professional in the field of DevOps advisory services and the essence of her experience is well-captured in the book.

Mukundan TN, CEO and Founder, Relevance Infosystems Pvt. Ltd.

This book is like having enough wood to burn a campfire during winter in the Arctic! Urmila assembled a breadth-and-depth approach to DevOps assessment that covers what organizations of all sizes need to assess their state of DevOps, or lack of it. As a lean-agile enterprise transformation coach who works with large and small organizations, I see this playbook as a tool that saves assessment time and increases the resulting value by choosing the questions applicable to your situation.

Masa Maeda, CEO and Founder, Value Innova

As one who places tremendous value in businesses focused on transforming lives, I consider this book a "must read" in assessing DevOps for Technology Organizations. Urmila has once again hit the mark in providing exceptional tools that achieve the trip aim for improving people, process and technology.

Mike Fidgeon, Former CEO, Pathways by Molina